**GoodFood**

# 101 BEST EVER CURRIES

D0928449

10 9 8 7 6 5 4 3 2 1

Published in 2009 by BBC Books,
an imprint of Ebury Publishing
A Random House Group company

The Random House Group Limited
Reg. No. 954009

Addresses for companies within the
Random House Group can be found at
www.randomhouse.co.uk

A CIP catalogue record for this book is available
from the British Library.

The Random House Group Limited supports
The Forest Stewardship Council (FSC), the
leading international forest certification organization.
All our titles that are printed on Greenpeace
approved FSC certified paper carry the FSC logo.
Our paper procurement policy can be found at
www.rbooks.co.uk/environment

To buy books by your favourite authors and
register for offers visit www.rbooks.co.uk

Printed and bound by Firmengruppe APPL,
aprinta druck, Wemding, Germany
Colour origination by Dot Gradations Ltd, UK

Commissioning Editor: Muna Reyal
Project Editor: Joe Cottington
Designer: Annette Peppis
Production: Lucy Harrison
Picture Researcher: Gabby Harrington

ISBN: 9781846077661

**GoodFood**

# 101 BEST EVER CURRIES
## TRIPLE-TESTED RECIPES

Editor
**Sarah Cook**

# Contents

Introduction    6

# Introduction

Versatile and flavoursome, the popularity of curries has grown and grown, and they're now a favourite among our readers, who are always asking the *Good Food* team for more. So, what's our solution? Pick our favourites and put them all into one useful little book.

From quick supper ideas using a few store-cupboard ingredients to elaborate dishes cooked from scratch that are perfect for impressing friends, we've included Thai, Indian and Caribbean varieties, plus some low-fat and healthy recipes for those watching their waistline. But this book isn't just about the main event; we've also included some delicious side dishes and desserts, so you'll have everything you need. Plus each one has been tested by the team at the magazine, so you know they will work for you.

Most of these recipes feed a family of four, but curries are easily doubled if you're feeding a crowd and taste even better second time around if there are only two of you, as the flavours develop beautifully. Work your way through the chapters, cooking up classics and experimenting with some of the more unusual ideas – from a creamy *Chicken korma* to *Red prawns with chilli and lime leaf*. So bin the takeaway menu, grab those spices and get cooking!

*Sarah*

Sarah Cook
*Good Food* magazine

# Notes and conversion tables

## NOTES ON THE RECIPES
• Eggs are large in the UK and Australia and extra large in America unless stated otherwise.
• Wash fresh produce before preparation.
• Recipes contain nutritional analyses for 'sugar', which means the total sugar content including all natural sugars in the ingredients, unless otherwise stated.

## OVEN TEMPERATURES

| Gas | °C | °C Fan | °F | Oven temp. |
|-----|-----|--------|-----|----------------|
| ¼   | 110 | 90     | 225 | Very cool      |
| ½   | 120 | 100    | 250 | Very cool      |
| 1   | 140 | 120    | 275 | Cool or slow   |
| 2   | 150 | 130    | 300 | Cool or slow   |
| 3   | 160 | 140    | 325 | Warm           |
| 4   | 180 | 160    | 350 | Moderate       |
| 5   | 190 | 170    | 375 | Moderately hot |
| 6   | 200 | 180    | 400 | Fairly hot     |
| 7   | 220 | 200    | 425 | Hot            |
| 8   | 230 | 210    | 450 | Very hot       |
| 9   | 240 | 220    | 475 | Very hot       |

## APPROXIMATE WEIGHT CONVERSIONS
• All the recipes in this book list both imperial and metric measurements. Conversions are approximate and have been rounded up or down. Follow one set of measurements only; do not mix the two.
• Cup measurements, which are used by cooks in Australia and America, have not been listed here as they vary from ingredient to ingredient. Kitchen scales should be used to measure dry/solid ingredients.

*Good Food* are concerned about sustainable sourcing and animal welfare so where possible, we use organic ingredients, humanely-reared meats, free-range chickens and eggs and unrefined sugar.

SPOON MEASURES

Spoon measurements are level unless otherwise specified.

- 1 teaspoon (tsp) = 5ml
- 1 tablespoon (tbsp) = 15ml
- 1 Australian tablespoon = 20ml (cooks in Australia should measure 3 teaspoons where 1 tablespoon is specified in a recipe)

APPROXIMATE LIQUID CONVERSIONS

| metric | imperial | AUS | US |
|--------|----------|-----|-----|
| 50ml | 2fl oz | ¼ cup | ¼ cup |
| 125ml | 4fl oz | ½ cup | ½ cup |
| 175ml | 6fl oz | ¾ cup | ¾ cup |
| 225ml | 8fl oz | 1 cup | 1 cup |
| 300ml | 10fl oz/½ pint | ½ pint | 1¼ cups |
| 450ml | 16fl oz | 2 cups | 2 cups/1 pint |
| 600ml | 20fl oz/1 pint | 1 pint | 2½ cups |
| 1 litre | 35fl oz/1¾ pints | 1¾ pints | 1 quart |

Thai curry paste can vary in temperature from fairly mild to very hot, depending on the brand. If you're using an authentic Thai label, add 1 teaspoon at first, then more to taste.

# Thai red salmon curry

1 tsp vegetable or sunflower oil
1 tbsp Thai red curry paste
1 onion, sliced
250ml/9fl oz reduced-fat coconut milk
2 × 250g skinless salmon fillets, cut into chunks
200g/8oz trimmed green beans
a few fresh coriander leaves, to garnish
rice, to serve

Takes 15 minutes • Serves 4

1 Heat the oil in a large pan, then add the curry paste. Stir in the onion and cook for about 5 minutes until softened. Pour in the coconut milk and bring to the boil.
2 Reduce to a simmer, then add the salmon chunks and beans. Leave to simmer gently for 5 minutes until the fish flakes easily and the beans are tender. Scatter with the coriander and serve with rice.

• Per serving 326 kcalories, protein 27g, carbohydrate 5g, fat 22g, saturated fat 9g, fibre 2g, sugar 4g, salt 0.46g

This dish is like a Thai version of a pilaf; try adding baby sweetcorn when in season for extra crunch.

# Oven-baked Thai chicken rice

1 tbsp vegetable oil
1 onion, chopped
400g pack mini chicken fillets
4 tbsp Thai green curry paste
250g/9oz basmati and wild rice mix, rinsed
2 red peppers, seeded and cut into wedges
finely grated zest and juice of 1 lime
400ml can reduced-fat coconut milk
a handful of fresh coriander leaves, to serve

Takes 30 minutes • Serves 4

1  Preheat the oven to 200°C/180°C fan/gas 6.
2  Heat the oil in a shallow ovenproof casserole dish over a medium heat. Tip in the onion and soften for 5 minutes. Increase the heat, add the chicken and curry paste, and cook for 2 minutes, stirring to coat.
3  Tip in the rice and peppers, then stir in the lime zest and juice, coconut milk and 250ml/8fl oz boiling water. Bring to the boil, then pop the lid on and bake in the oven for 20 minutes until the rice is fluffy. Scatter with coriander before serving.

• Per serving 510 kcalories, protein 32g, carbohydrate 59g, fat 18g, saturated fat 10g, fibre 2g, sugar 8g, salt 1.02g

If you don't like chickpeas, simply swap them for a can of red lentils, which will also help the sauce thicken nicely.

## Chicken and chickpea curry

4 tbsp vegetable oil
400g/14oz chicken breast, cut into chunks
2 onions, sliced
2 tbsp medium curry powder
425ml/¾ pint chicken stock
410g can chickpeas, drained and rinsed
2 tbsp natural yogurt
rice, to serve

Takes 30 minutes • Serves 4

1 Heat 2 tablespoons of the oil in a frying pan, then add the chicken chunks and fry for a few minutes to brown, stirring. Remove the chicken, tip half the onions into the pan and cook for 5 minutes until softened. Return the chicken with the curry powder, and stir for a couple of minutes until the chicken and onions are coated in the spice.
2 Pour in the stock and chickpeas, bring to the boil then simmer, covered, for 10 minutes until the chicken is almost cooked through.
3 Meanwhile, heat the remaining oil in a separate pan, add the rest of the onions and fry over a high heat for 5 minutes until crisp and brown. Drain on kitchen paper.
4 Stir the yogurt into the curry and bubble for a few minutes, uncovered. Serve with rice, scattered with the crispy onions.

• Per serving 341 kcalories, protein 31g, carbohydrate 20g, fat 16g, saturated fat 2g, fibre 6g, sugar 4g, salt 1.47g

If you're watching your calorie intake, make a lighter version by using half the amount of coconut milk topped up with 200ml/8fl oz vegetable or chicken stock.

# Sweet and spicy fish

3 tbsp medium curry paste
1 large onion, halved and sliced
1 red pepper, seeded and thickly sliced
1 small bunch of fresh coriander, leaves and stems separated and roughly chopped
400ml can reduced-fat coconut milk
a large handful of dried mango pieces, chopped
700g/1lb 9oz firm skinless white fish fillets, cut into large chunks
naan breads, to serve

Takes 25 minutes • Serves 4

1  Heat the curry paste in a large pan and fry the onion for 3 minutes until starting to soften. Stir in the sliced pepper and coriander stems, and cook for another 2 minutes. Pour in the coconut milk, tip in the mango pieces and bring to the boil. Season to taste, turn down the heat and simmer for 5 minutes until slightly thickened.
2  Add the fish and cook for 3–5 minutes or until it flakes easily. Sprinkle the coriander leaves over the curry just before serving with warmed naan breads.

• Per serving 332 kcalories, protein 35g, carbohydrate 18g, fat 14g, saturated fat 9g, fibre 2g, added sugar none, salt 1g

To make a tasty yogurt sauce, mix 200g/8oz low-fat natural yogurt with 1 teaspoon of ground turmeric and 2 tablespoons of chopped fresh mint leaves.

# Chickpea curry roll-ups

1 tbsp olive oil
2 onions, sliced
a thumb-sized knob of ginger, grated
1 tbsp garam masala
400g can cherry tomatoes
410g can chickpeas, drained
500g bag spinach leaves
8 chapatis
natural yogurt, to serve (optional)

Takes 20 minutes • Serves 4

1 Heat the oil in a large frying pan, then gently cook the onions and ginger for 5 minutes until beginning to soften. Stir in the spice, cook for 1 minute, then add the tomatoes and chickpeas. Fill the tomato can one-third full with water, tip this in too, then bubble for 5 minutes until the sauce has thickened a little. Stir in three-quarters of the spinach leaves, a handful at a time, then warm through for a few minutes.
2 Heat the chapatis in the microwave, following the packet instructions. Serve the curry spooned over the warm chapatis, with the remaining spinach and a dollop of yogurt, if you like.

• Per serving (with yogurt) 424 kcalories, protein 19g, carbohydrate 64g, fat 12g, saturated fat 2g, fibre 7g, sugar 14g, salt 1.81g

No curry book is complete without a recipe using Christmas leftovers, and if you're out of parsnips, try swapping with potatoes, peas or carrots – just no Brussels sprouts!

# Turkey and parsnip curry

2 tbsp vegetable oil
2 onions, halved and thinly sliced
500g/1lb 2oz parsnips, peeled and cut into chunks
4 tbsp madras curry paste
400g can chopped tomatoes
500g/1lb 2oz cooked turkey, cut into chunks
150g pot low-fat natural yogurt
basmati rice, to serve

Takes 30 minutes • Serves 4

1  Heat the oil in a pan, add the onions and parsnips, and fry for 10 minutes until they are softened and lightly coloured.
2  Stir in the curry paste, then add the tomatoes with a little salt and stir well. Fill the can with water, tip it in and bring to the boil. Cover and simmer for 10 minutes, until the parsnips are almost tender.
3  Stir in the turkey chunks, cover the pan again and simmer for a further 5 minutes until the turkey is heated through. Lightly swirl through the yogurt and serve with basmati rice.

• Per serving 406 kcalories, protein 43g, carbohydrate 27g, fat 15g, saturated fat 2g, fibre 8g, added sugar none, salt 1.22g

A milder curry paste, such as korma or tikka, works well in this recipe, but if you like things spicier, notch up the heat a bit with some madras paste.

# Coconut jinga

2 tbsp vegetable oil
1 onion, chopped
1 tsp finely chopped ginger
2 tbsp mild curry paste
85g/3oz creamed coconut
2 tomatoes, roughly chopped
1 tsp tomato purée
2 tsp fresh lemon juice
500g/1lb 2oz cooked shelled prawns
basmati rice, 1 tbsp dessicated coconut and fresh chopped coriander, to serve

Takes 20 minutes • Serves 4

1  Heat the oil in a large frying pan and fry the onion and ginger until soft. Stir in the curry paste and gently fry for 2 minutes. Put the creamed coconut in a small bowl, then stir in 150ml/¼ pint hot water until smooth. Stir into the onion.

2  Add the tomatoes, tomato purée and lemon juice, and salt to taste. Simmer for 5 minutes, adding the prawns for the last 2 minutes to heat through. Serve on a bed of rice, sprinkled with dessicated coconut and a little chopped coriander.

• Per serving 285 kcalories, protein 30g, carbohydrate 6g, fat 16g, saturated fat 7g, fibre 1g, added sugar none, salt 2.19g

This is a delicious and filling vegetable curry, but if you are serving it to vegetarians, make sure the curry paste is suitable.

# One-pot mushroom and potato curry

1 tbsp oil
1 onion, roughly chopped
1 large potato, chopped into small chunks
1 aubergine, trimmed and chopped into chunks
250g/9oz button mushrooms
2–4 tbsp balti curry paste (depending on how hot you like it)
150ml/¼ pint vegetable stock
400ml can reduced-fat coconut milk
chopped fresh coriander and rice or naan bread, to serve

Takes 30 minutes • Serves 4

1  Heat the oil in a large pan, add the onion and potato. Cover, then cook over a low heat for 5 minutes until the potato starts to soften. Throw in the aubergine and mushrooms, then cook for a few more minutes.
2  Stir in the curry paste, pour over the stock and coconut milk. Bring to the boil, then simmer for 10 minutes or until the potato is tender. Scatter with the coriander and serve with rice or naan bread.

• Per serving 212 kcalories, protein 5g, carbohydrate 15g, fat 15g, saturated fat 9g, fibre 3g, sugar 5g, salt 0.71g

A perfect after-work curry for two – 5 minutes chopping then 10 minutes in the pan.

# No-fry Thai curry

2 rounded tbsp Thai green curry paste
400ml can coconut milk
2 skinless chicken breast fillets, very thinly sliced
1 red pepper, seeded and cut into chunks
3 spring onions, halved lengthways and cut into long pieces
2 handfuls of frozen peas
2 tbsp chopped fresh coriander
rice or noodles, to serve

Takes 15 minutes • Serves 2

1 In a medium pan, stir the curry paste over the heat for a few seconds, then pour in the coconut milk and bring to the boil.

2 Add the chicken and veg, let everything start to bubble again, then turn down the heat and cook very gently for 5 minutes until the chicken is tender but the vegetables still have some crunch. Stir in the coriander and serve spooned over rice or noodles.

• Per serving 544 kcalories, protein 40g, carbohydrate 15g, fat 40g, saturated fat 30g, fibre 4g, sugar 12g, salt 1.88g

Kids love this curry because of the bright colours and the flavour of the sweet potatoes; it's easily doubled if you're feeding a crowd.

# Sweet potato and pea curry

3 tbsp curry paste from a jar (use your favourite)
1 onion, finely chopped
450g/1lb potatoes, cut into chunks
2 large sweet potatoes (about 900g/2lb), cut into chunks
600ml/1 pint vegetable stock
400ml can coconut milk
175g/6oz frozen peas
few fresh coriander sprigs, roughly chopped, to garnish

Takes 30 minutes • Serves 4

1 Heat the curry paste in a large pan and stir in the onion. Cover and cook for 5 minutes, stirring occasionally, until softened. Add all the potatoes, the stock and coconut milk to the pan and bring to the boil.
2 Turn the heat down and simmer the curry for 20 minutes until the potato has softened, adding the peas for the final 2 minutes. Season to taste and spoon the curry into bowls, scattering over the coriander before you tuck in.

• Per serving 513 kcalories, protein 11g, carbohydrate 77g, fat 20g, saturated fat 14g, fibre 10g, added sugar none, salt 1.46g

Rinsing basmati rice removes some of the starch that can make a pilaf sticky, not light and fluffy.

# One-pan prawn pilaf

2 tbsp korma curry paste
1 small onion, finely chopped
1 red chilli, seeded and sliced into rings
300g/10oz basmati rice, drained and rinsed
700ml/1¼ pints chicken stock
140g/5oz cooked peeled prawns, defrosted if frozen
a cupful of frozen peas
a handful of fresh coriander leaves, chopped, to garnish
lemon wedges, to serve

Takes 25 minutes • Serves 4

1  Heat a large wide pan and dry-fry the curry paste, onion and most of the chilli for 4–5 minutes until the onion begins to soften. Add the rice, stirring to coat in the curry paste, then add the stock and bring to the boil.

2  Cover the pan and lower the heat. Leave the rice to simmer slowly for 12–15 minutes until all the liquid has been absorbed and the rice is cooked. Turn off the heat and stir in the prawns and peas. Cover the pan and leave to stand for 5 minutes.

3  Fluff up the rice grains with a fork and season, if you like. Scatter over the coriander and remaining chilli, and serve with lemon wedges.

• Per serving 340 kcalories, protein 18g, carbohydrate 65g, fat 3g, saturated fat 1g, fibre 2g, added sugar none, salt 2.38g

Quick and colourful, this variation on a classic will fill up the whole family.

# Indian 'beans on toast'

2 tbsp vegetable oil
2 medium onions, cut into thin wedges
1 tsp ground turmeric
1 rounded tsp ground cumin
4 medium tomatoes, cut into rough chunks
410g can green lentils, drained and rinsed
4 plain or garlic and coriander, naan breads
a handful of fresh coriander leaves, roughly torn
a few dollops of natural yogurt, to garnish
lemon wedges, to serve

Takes 20 minutes • Serves 4

1 Heat the oil in a frying pan. Tip in the onions and cook until really golden, about 5–8 minutes. Stir in the turmeric and cumin for a minute, then add the tomatoes and cook briefly, moving them around in the pan until they just start to soften but don't lose their shape.

2 Tip in the lentils and heat through for a minute or so. While they are warming, tear the naan breads roughly in half and toast them under the grill or in the toaster – just to warm them through and soften but not brown.

3 Stir 3–4 tablespoons of water into the lentils to make a little sauce, warm through, then stir in the coriander and some seasoning. Spoon the lentils over the naan, top with a dollop of yogurt, and add a lemon wedge on the side for squeezing over.

• Per serving 440 kcalories, protein 14g, carbohydrate 64g, fat 16g, saturated fat 6g, fibre 5g, added sugar 2g, salt 1.05g

If you don't have any cashew nuts, just stir in a couple of spoonfuls of crunchy peanut butter at the end to give it a satay flavour.

# Thai red squash curry

1 small butternut squash (about 700g/1lb 9oz)
2 tbsp sunflower oil
1–2 tbsp Thai red curry paste, depending on your taste
400ml can coconut milk
150ml/¼ pint vegetable stock
2 tbsp soy sauce
1 tbsp light muscovado sugar
200g pack mixed baby corn and mangetout, corn halved lengthways
juice of ½ lime
a handful of roasted cashew nuts

Takes 30 minutes • Serves 4

1 Cut off the ends of the squash, quarter lengthways, scoop out fibres and seeds, peel, then cut into small chunks.
2 Heat the oil in a pan. Fry the curry paste and squash chunks for 3 minutes. Add the coconut milk, stock, soy sauce and sugar, and bring to the boil.
3 Add the corn and simmer, covered, for around 10–12 minutes. When the squash is tender add the mangetout and lime juice, and simmer for a final minute. Stir in the nuts, taste and season.

• Per serving 283 kcalories, protein 4.4g, carbohydrate 16.2g, fat 22.6g, saturated fat 14.6g, fibre 2.2g, added sugar 5.3g, salt 1.95g

A laksa is a curried noodle soup from Malaysia that can be made with vegetables, tofu, chicken, fish, seafood – whatever takes your fancy. This spicy one features succulent prawns.

# Spicy prawn laksa

1 tbsp sunflower oil
300g bag mixed crunchy stir-fry vegetables
140g/5oz shiitake mushrooms, sliced
2 tbsp Thai green curry paste
400ml can reduced-fat coconut milk
200ml/7fl oz vegetable or fish stock
300g/10oz medium straight-to-wok noodles
200g/8oz large raw peeled prawns

Takes 20 minutes • Serves 4

1 Heat a wok, add the oil, then stir-fry the mixed veg and mushrooms for 2–3 minutes. Remove and set aside.
2 Tip the curry paste into the pan and fry for 1 minute. Pour in the coconut milk and stock. Bring to the boil, drop in the noodles and prawns, then reduce the heat and simmer for 4 minutes until the prawns are cooked through. Stir the veg and mushrooms back in, then serve ladled into bowls.

• Per serving 327 kcalories, protein 16g, carbohydrate 32g, fat 17g, saturated fat 10g, fibre 4g, sugar 4g, salt 0.97g

When you find cumin in a recipe it's often hand-in-hand with coriander; their flavours really complement each other, and particularly so in this four-spice curry.

# Four-spice lamb curry

2 tbsp sunflower oil
1 large onion, very finely chopped
1 tsp each chilli flakes and ground ginger
2 tsp each ground coriander and cumin
500g/1lb 2oz lean lamb neck fillet, cubed
1 large red pepper, seeded and cubed
1 lamb stock cube
3 tomatoes, cut into wedges
410g can chickpeas, drained
a little chopped fresh coriander, to garnish (optional)

Takes 30 minutes • Serves 4

1  Heat the oil in a wok, then fry the onion for about 4 minutes until soft. Stir in the spices, reserving 1 teaspoon of cumin, then fry for a few seconds more. Toss in the lamb and pepper, and stir-fry over a high heat until the meat has browned.

2  Stir in 200ml/7fl oz water, crumble in the stock cube, season well, then cover and cook for about 6 minutes until the mixture is pulpy and the meat tender. Stir in the tomatoes, chickpeas and remaining spoonful of cumin, and heat through for 2 minutes. If the sauce is too thick, add a splash of water to thin it a little. Serve scattered with the coriander, if using.

• Per serving 439 kcalories, protein 31g, carbohydrate 21g, fat 26g, saturated fat 10g, fibre 5g, added sugar none, salt 0.47g

A lovely winter warmer to serve with hot naan bread or chapatis on the side.

# Curried corn and coconut soup

25g/1oz butter
1 onion, chopped
1 garlic clove, chopped
½ thumb-sized knob of ginger, chopped
2 tbsp hot madras curry paste or powder
600ml/1 pint chicken stock
400ml can coconut milk
2 × 300g cans sweetcorn, drained
2 tbsp Greek yogurt, 1 tsp garam masala and fresh coriander, to garnish

Takes 30 minutes • Serves 4–6

1 Melt the butter in a pan over a low heat and cook the onion, garlic and ginger until soft. Add the curry paste or powder and stir for 2 minutes. Pour in the stock, coconut milk, half the sweetcorn and some seasoning. Bring to the boil, reduce the heat and simmer for 10 minutes.

2 Pour the soup into a food processor or blender and blend until smooth. Return to the pan, stir in the remaining sweetcorn and heat through. Ladle into bowls, swirl with yogurt, dust with garam masala and garnish with a little coriander.

• Per serving (4) 403 kcalories, protein 7g, carbohydrate 39g, fat 25g, saturated fat 18g, fibre 2g, added sugar 9g, salt 2.04g

It's important to fry your spices before adding any liquid; that way they will release maximum flavour into the dish.

# Creamy egg curry

2 tbsp oil
1 large or 2 medium onions, thinly sliced
2 heaped tbsp mild or medium curry paste
½ × 400g can tomatoes
8 eggs
140g/5oz frozen peas
4 tbsp Greek yogurt
rice and mango chutney, to serve

Takes 25 minutes • Serves 4

1 Heat the oil in a frying pan. Add the onion and fry for 5 minutes until golden. Add the curry paste and cook, stirring, for 2 minutes. Add the tomatoes, 200ml/7fl oz water and a little salt and pepper. Bring to the boil, then reduce the heat and simmer for 10 minutes until the onions are softened. Add a splash of water if the curry becomes too thick.
2 Meanwhile, bring a pan of water to the boil. Carefully lower in the eggs and simmer for 8 minutes. Do not boil too hard, as this will make the eggs tough.
3 Stir the peas and yogurt into the curry. Simmer for 2–3 minutes. Cool the eggs under cold running water. Peel and halve each egg and gently stir into the curry. Serve with rice and mango chutney.

• Per serving 302 kcalories, protein 18g, carbohydrate 12g, fat 21g, saturated fat 5g, fibre 3g, added sugar none, salt 0.84g

If you've got a bit more time to spare, simmer the chicken thighs for 30–40 minutes before adding the cabbage; they'll become lovely and tender.

## 30-minute chicken curry

1 large or 2 medium onions, chopped
2 tbsp vegetable oil
500g/1lb 2oz boneless, skinless chicken thighs
2 tbsp tikka paste
425ml/¾ pint vegetable stock
2 potatoes, peeled and cubed
1 tbsp tomato purée
6-8 cabbage leaves, shredded

Takes 30 minutes • Serves 4

1 Fry the onions in the oil for 5 mins until soft and browning. Add the chicken and fry until lightly coloured. Stir in the curry paste for a minute, followed by the stock, potatoes and tomato purée. Season and bring to the boil.
2 Reduce the heat and cover. Simmer for 15 minutes. Stir in the cabbage and cook for 5 minutes more.

• Per serving 297 kcalories, protein 30g, carbohydrate 20g, fat 11g, saturated fat 2g, fibre 3g, added sugar none, salt 0.97g

A light curry that's perfect for spring or summer eating.

# New potato and mince curry

450g/1lb minced turkey
1 tbsp vegetable oil
1 small onion, chopped
3 garlic cloves, finely chopped
1 tbsp coarsely grated ginger
1 fresh red chilli, seeded and finely sliced
2 tsp each ground cumin and coriander
1 tbsp korma curry paste
500g/1lb 2oz new potatoes, halved
100g/4oz fresh spinach
150g/5oz Greek yogurt
chapatis or naan bread, to serve

Takes 1 hour • Serves 4

1 Heat a frying pan and dry-fry the mince. Brown it all over, stirring to break it up. Remove from the pan and set aside. Add the oil and onion to the pan, and cook for 5 minutes.
2 Stir in the garlic, ginger, chilli, spices and curry paste. Stir-fry for 1 minute. Add the mince, potatoes and 600ml/1 pint water, bring to the boil, cover, then simmer for 30 minutes. Season with salt to taste.
3 Stir in the spinach and simmer for 1 minute, uncovered, until wilted. Swirl through the yogurt and serve with Indian bread.

• Per serving 315 kcalories, protein 32g, carbohydrate 25g, fat 10g, saturated fat 3g, fibre 2g, sugar 4g, salt 0.55g

Packed full of lentils, vegetables and dried fruit, you won't be left feeling hungry after this low-fat curry.

# Easy-peasy lentil curry

2 tbsp sunflower oil
2 medium onions, cut into rough wedges
4 tbsp curry paste
850ml/1½ pints vegetable stock
750g/1lb 10oz mixed veg (such as carrots, parsnips and sweet potatoes), peeled and cut into small chunks
100g/4oz red lentils
200g/8oz basmati rice
¼ tsp ground turmeric
a handful of raisins
a handful of roughly chopped fresh parsley
poppadums and mango chutney, to serve

Takes 40–50 minutes • Serves 4

1 Heat the oil in a large pan. Add the onions and cook over a high heat for about 8 minutes or until golden brown. Stir in the curry paste for a minute then pour in a little of the stock so it sizzles, scraping any bits from the bottom of the pan. Pour in the rest of the stock.
2 Stir in the vegetables, cover and simmer for 5 minutes. Add the lentils and simmer for a further 15–20 minutes or until cooked.
3 While the curry is simmering, cook the rice according to the packet instructions, adding the turmeric to the cooking water. Drain well.
4 Season the curry, toss in the raisins and the chopped parsley, then serve with the rice, and some poppadums and chutney.

• Per serving 432 kcalories, protein 14g, carbohydrate 76g, fat 10g, saturated fat 1g, fibre 6g, added sugar none, salt 1.38g

This superhealthy recipe is great for vegetarians as it is packed full of spinach, which is a good source of iron.

# Tamarind chickpeas

1 tbsp vegetable or sunflower oil
½ tsp kalonji seeds (also known as onion or nigella seeds)
1 tsp fennel seeds
1 medium onion, chopped
400g can chopped tomatoes
3 green chillies, seeded and cut into quarters lengthways
2–3 tsp light muscovado sugar
1 tsp each paprika and ground turmeric
410g can chickpeas, drained and rinsed
1 tbsp tamarind paste
1 tbsp chopped coriander
½ × 250g bag baby leaf spinach
natural yogurt and chapatis, to serve

Takes 25–35 minutes • Serves 2

1  Heat the oil in a pan, fry the kalonji and fennel seeds for about 10 seconds. Add the onion and cook gently for 8–10 minutes until lightly golden.
2  Mix in the tomatoes, chillies, sugar, paprika, turmeric and chickpeas. Bring to the boil, then simmer for 10 minutes. Stir in the tamarind and coriander. Add the spinach leaves and stir gently until they've just wilted. Serve with yogurt and chapatis.

• Per serving 334 kcalories, protein 16g, carbohydrate 45g, fat 11g, saturated fat 1g, fibre 9g, added sugar 5g, salt 1.34g

By whizzing the ingredients to a paste first, they can cook without needing oil.

# Fragrant chicken curry with chickpeas

2 onions, quartered
3 fat garlic cloves
½ × finger-length knob of ginger, roughly chopped
2 tbsp medium curry powder
½ tsp ground turmeric
2 tsp paprika
1 fresh red chilli, seeded and roughly chopped
1 small bunch of fresh coriander
425ml/¾ pint chicken stock
4 skinless chicken breasts, cubed
410g can chickpeas, drained and rinsed
low-fat natural yogurt, rice and microwaved poppadums, to serve

Takes 1 hour • Serves 4

1  Tip the onions, garlic, ginger, ground spices, chilli and half the coriander into a food processor. Add 1 teaspoon of salt and blend to a purée. Tip the mixture into a pan and cook over a low heat for 10 minutes, stirring frequently.
2  Pour in the stock and bring to the boil. Add the chicken, then lower the heat and simmer for 20 minutes until tender.
3  Chop the remaining coriander and stir most of it into the curry with the chickpeas. Heat through. Sprinkle with the reserved coriander, and serve with yogurt, rice and microwaved poppadums.

• Per serving 272 kcalories, protein 39g, carbohydrate 19g, fat 5g, saturated fat 1g, fibre 5g, added sugar none, salt 1.68g

Lentils contain useful amounts of zinc, iron and calcium as well as cholesterol-lowering fibre; combine them with peas and you will increase the quantity of iron you absorb.

# Spiced rice and lentils with cauliflower

2 tbsp sunflower oil
1 onion, chopped
2 carrots, chopped
200g/8oz basmati rice
50g/2oz red lentils
3 rounded tbsp korma curry paste
1 cauliflower, cut into florets
100g/4oz frozen peas
a few toasted cashew nuts, to garnish
natural yogurt and mango chutney, to serve

Takes 45 minutes • Serves 4

1 Heat the oil in a pan, add the onion and carrots, then fry for 5 minutes until lightly coloured. Stir in the rice and lentils, cook for 1 more minute, add the curry paste and 900ml/1½ pints water, then bring to the boil. Cover, then simmer for 10 minutes.
2 Stir in the cauliflower, then cook for 10 minutes more until the rice and lentils are tender. Add the peas 2 minutes before the cooking time is up, stirring them through. Top with the nuts, then serve with yogurt and mango chutney in bowls.

• Per serving 404 kcalories, protein 16g, carbohydrate 62g, fat 12g, saturated fat 1g, fibre 7g, sugar 11g, salt 0.81g

This low-fat curry can be on the table in only 15 minutes from scratch.

# Super-quick fish curry

1 tbsp vegetable oil
1 large onion, chopped
1 garlic clove, chopped
1–2 tbsp madras curry paste
400g can chopped tomatoes
200ml/7fl oz vegetable stock
600g/1lb 5oz white fish fillet, skinned and cut into big chunks
rice or naan bread, to serve

Takes 15 minutes • Serves 4

1 Heat the oil in a deep pan and gently fry the onion and garlic for about 5 minutes until soft. Add the curry paste and stir-fry for 1–2 minutes, then tip in the tomatoes and stock.
2 Bring to a simmer, then add the fish. Gently cook for 4–5 minutes until the fish flakes easily. Serve immediately with rice or naan bread.

• Per serving 191 kcalories, protein 30g, carbohydrate 8g, fat 5g, saturated fat 1g, fibre 2g, sugar 6g, salt 0.54g

Not only is this curry healthy, it also uses up leftover cooked chicken – perfect for a Monday-night dinner.

# Fruity chicken and coconut curry

200g/8oz long grain, Thai or basmati rice
1 tbsp sunflower oil
2 courgettes, cut into chunks
1 red pepper, seeded and cut into chunks
375g/13oz skinless cooked chicken, chopped into chunks
1 bunch of spring onions, finely sliced
100ml/3½fl oz reduced-fat coconut milk
150ml/¼ pint chicken stock
1 tbsp Thai red curry paste
1 orange, segmented

Takes 35 minutes • Serves 4

1  Cook the rice in boiling water according to the packet instructions.

2  Meanwhile, heat the oil in a wok or large frying pan and add the courgettes and pepper. Stir-fry over a high heat for 3 minutes until just starting to brown. Add the chicken and cook, stirring, for 2 minutes.

3  Toss in the spring onions and pour over the coconut milk, stock and curry paste. Heat until simmering then cook, uncovered, for 5–6 minutes.

4  Add the orange segments to the chicken mixture. Heat for 1–2 minutes, then season. Drain the rice and divide it and the curry among four warmed plates.

• Per serving 445 kcalories, protein 30g, carbohydrate 58g, fat 11g, saturated fat 4g, fibre 2g, added sugar none, salt 0.8g

You don't have to avoid pork if you're trying to eat healthily, just choose a leaner cut, such as the fillet.

# Spicy pork and aubergine curry

4 tsp olive oil
2 onions, sliced
1 aubergine, diced
500g/1lb 2oz lean pork fillet, trimmed of any fat and sliced
2 red peppers, seeded and cut into chunky strips
2–3 tbsp mild curry powder
400g can plum tomatoes
basmati rice, to serve

Takes 40 minutes • Serves 4

1 Heat the oil in a large non-stick frying pan with a lid. Tip in the onions and aubergine, and fry for 8 minutes, stirring frequently, until soft and golden brown.

2 Tip in the pork and fry for 5 minutes, stirring occasionally, until starting to brown. Mix in the pepper strips and stir-fry for about 3 minutes until soft.

3 Sprinkle in the curry powder. Stir-fry for a minute, then pour in the tomatoes and 150ml/¼ pint water. Stir vigorously, cover the pan and leave the mixture to simmer for 5 minutes until the tomatoes break down to form a thick sauce – you can add a drop more water if the mixture gets too thick. Season with salt and pepper, and serve with basmati rice.

• Per serving 293 kcalories, protein 31g, carbohydrate 16g, fat 11g, saturated fat 2g, fibre 6g, added sugar none, salt 0.4g

This curry has all the flavour of a korma without the rich, creamy sauce.

# Low-fat prawn and almond korma

1 tbsp sunflower oil
1 onion, chopped
400g pack frozen raw peeled prawns, defrosted
2 tbsp korma curry paste
3 tbsp ground almonds
a handful of fresh coriander leaves, roughly chopped, to garnish
rice, to serve

Takes 20 minutes • Serves 4

1  Heat the oil in a frying pan, add the onion, then fry for 5 minutes until lightly coloured.
2  Add the prawns, then stir quickly until they are evenly pink. Stir in the curry paste, then add 150ml/¼ pint water and the ground almonds. Bring to the boil, then simmer for 2–3 minutes until the sauce is slightly thickened. Scatter with the chopped coriander and serve with rice.

• Per serving 188 kcalories, protein 21g, carbohydrate 4g, fat 10g, saturated fat 1g, fibre 1g, sugar 2g, salt 0.8g

Just one portion of this curry provides all five of your 5-a-day target.

# Squash, spinach and black bean dopiaza

2 onions, thinly sliced
2 tbsp sunflower oil
1 garlic clove, crushed
1 tsp each ground cumin, ground coriander and curry powder
a pinch of chilli powder
400g/14oz butternut squash (peeled weight), cut into chunks
1 tbsp tomato purée
410g can black beans in water, drained and rinsed
200g/8oz fresh spinach, washed

Takes 40 minutes • Serves 2

1  Preheat the oven to 190°C/170°C fan/ gas 5.
2  Toss half the onions in 1 tablespoon of the oil, then tip into a roasting tin and roast in the oven for 15–20 minutes until crisp and golden.
3  Meanwhile, fry the remaining onion in the rest of the oil until lightly golden. Add the garlic and spices, and cook for 1 minute. Add the squash, stir in the tomato purée and 425ml/¾ pint boiling water, then return to the boil. Simmer, covered, for 15 minutes, then stir in the beans. Cook for a further 5 minutes.
4  Put the spinach in a colander and pour over a kettle of boiling water until wilted. Press with a wooden spoon to remove excess water, then roughly chop. Stir into the curry, then warm through. Serve scattered with the crisp roasted onions.

• Per serving 354 kcalories, protein 17g, carbohydrate 42g, fat 14g, saturated fat 2g, fibre 13g, sugar 14g, salt 0.51g

You can grate and chop your own ginger and chillies, if you like, but this is a curry for someone in a hurry.

# Low-fat chicken curry

1 tbsp sunflower oil
1 red onion, thinly sliced
1 garlic clove, crushed
2 tsp ready-prepared ginger, from a jar
½–1 tsp ready-chopped chillies, from a jar
½ × 400g can chopped tomatoes
200g/8oz skinless chicken breasts, chopped into chunks
2 tsp garam masala
3 tbsp low-fat natural yogurt, plus extra to serve (optional)
a handful of fresh coriander leaves, roughly chopped, to garnish
garlic and coriander naans, plus cucumber, lettuce and red onion salad, to serve

Takes 15 minutes • Serves 2

1 Heat the oil in a pan, add the onion and fry until softened. Add the garlic, ginger and chilli, and cook briefly. Add the tomatoes and a quarter of the can of water and bring to the boil. Simmer for 2 minutes, then add the chicken and garam masala, cover and cook for another 6–8 minutes until the chicken is cooked through.
2 Reduce the heat to a simmer, then stir in the yogurt. Sprinkle with coriander and serve with an extra spoon of yogurt, if you like, alongside warm garlic and coriander naans and a crisp salad of cucumber, shredded lettuce and sliced red onion.

• Per serving 248 kcalories, protein 29g, carbohydrate 16g, fat 8g, saturated fat 1g, fibre 3g, sugar 11g, salt 0.5g

This superhealthy curry is a real winter warmer.

# Winter root curry with lentils

2 tbsp sunflower or vegetable oil
1 onion, chopped
2 garlic cloves, crushed
700g/1lb 9oz potatoes, peeled and cut into chunks
4 carrots, peeled and thickly sliced
2 parsnips, peeled and thickly sliced
3 tbsp medium curry paste or powder
1 litre/1¾ pints vegetable stock
100g/4oz red lentils
1 small bunch of fresh coriander, roughly chopped
low-fat natural yogurt, to garnish
naan bread, to serve

Takes 40–45 minutes • Serves 4

1  Heat the oil in a large pan and cook the onion and garlic over a medium heat for 5 minutes until softened, stirring occasionally. Tip in the potatoes, carrots and parsnips, turn up the heat and cook for 6–7 minutes, stirring, until the vegetables are golden.
2  Stir in the curry paste or powder, pour in the stock and bring to the boil. Reduce the heat, add the lentils, cover and simmer for 15–20 minutes until the lentils and vegetables are tender and the sauce has thickened.
3  Stir in most of the coriander and some seasoning. Top with a dollop of yogurt and the remainder of the coriander. Serve with naan bread.

• Per serving 378 kcalories, protein 14g, carbohydrate 64g, fat 9g, saturated fat 1g, fibre 10g, added sugar none, salt 1.24g

A good source of vitamin C, this low-fat curry also counts for two of your 5-a-day target.

# Warming veggie curry

1 tbsp sunflower oil
1 butternut squash, peeled and cut into chunks
1 onion, sliced
1 tbsp Thai red curry paste
50g sachet creamed coconut
250g/9oz frozen French beans
warmed naan bread, to serve

Takes 35 minutes • Serves 4

1 Heat the oil in a pan. Tip in the squash and onion, then gently fry for about 5 minutes until the onion is soft, but not browned. Tip in the curry paste and cook for 1 minute more.
2 Mix the creamed coconut together with 300ml/½ pint boiling water, then pour into the pan. Bring to the boil and simmer for 10 minutes.
3 Add the beans to the pan, then cook for about 3–5 minutes more until everything is just tender. Serve with warmed naan bread.

• Per serving 178 kcalories, protein 5g, carbohydrate 23g, fat 9g, saturated fat 4g, fibre 5g, sugar 13g, salt 0.17g

A mild curry that gets its creaminess from a last-minute swirl of fromage frais.

# Light chicken korma

a small knob of ginger, finely sliced
1 garlic clove, crushed
1 onion, sliced
1 tbsp vegetable oil
4 skinless chicken breasts, cut into bite-sized pieces
1 tsp garam masala
100ml/3½fl oz chicken stock
3 tbsp low-fat fromage frais
2 tbsp ground almonds
a handful of toasted and sliced almonds and some chopped fresh coriander, to garnish
rice and chapatis or naan bread, to serve

Takes 35 minutes • Serves 4

1  Cook the ginger, garlic and onion in a large pan with the oil until softened. Tip in the chicken and cook until lightly browned, about 5 minutes, then add the garam masala and cook for 1 minute more. Pour over the stock and simmer for 10 minutes until the chicken is cooked through.

2  Mix together the fromage frais and ground almonds. Take the pan off the heat and stir in the fromage-frais mixture. Sprinkle over the sliced almonds, garnish with coriander and serve with rice and chapatis or plain naan bread, if you like.

• Per serving 243 kcalories, protein 37g, carbohydrate 4g, fat 9g, saturated fat 1g, fibre 1g, sugar 3g, salt 0.31g

Scoop this low-fat but hearty curry into bowls and eat with a spoon.

# Spiced chickpea and potato fry-up

300g/10oz potatoes, cut into
small pieces
2 onions, sliced
2 garlic cloves, crushed
1 tsp olive oil
1 tsp each ground coriander,
ground turmeric and mild
chilli powder
1 tbsp cumin seeds
410g can chickpeas, drained
and rinsed
2 tbsp tomato purée
200g/8oz baby leaf spinach
1 small bunch of freh coriander,
leaves chopped
wholemeal chapatis, low-fat natural
yogurt and mango chutney,
to serve

Takes 30 minutes • Serves 4

1  Boil the potatoes in a pan of salted water until just tender. While they are cooking, soften the onions and garlic in the oil in a frying pan for a few minutes. Add all the spices, then fry for 1 minute more. Stir in the chickpeas and tomato purée along with 400ml/14fl oz water, then turn up the heat and bubble for a few minutes.

2  When the potatoes are ready, drain them and add to the frying pan. Cook for a few minutes until the sauce is thick, stir in the spinach, then season.

3  When the spinach has wilted, stir in the coriander and serve with the chapatis, yogurt and chutney on the side.

• Per serving 201 kcalories, protein 10g, carbohydrate 33g, fat 4g, saturated fat none, fibre 6g, sugar 6g, salt 0.66g

Skinless chicken breast is very low in fat but can be expensive; if you're looking for a cheaper option, use skinless chicken thighs and just simmer them for 10–15 minutes more.

# Spicy autumn chicken

3 tbsp sunflower oil
3 skinless chicken breasts, cut into chunks
2 onions, sliced into wedges
3 tbsp mild curry paste
400g can chopped tomatoes
450g/1lb pumpkin or squash, peeled, seeded and cut into chunks
410g can chickpeas, drained and rinsed
warmed naan bread, to serve

Takes 30 minutes • Serves 4

1 Heat 2 tablespoons of the oil in a large pan and fry the chicken for 2–3 minutes until browned. Remove and set aside, draining off any excess liquid. Add the remaining oil to the pan, then fry the onions for 5 minutes until golden. Return the chicken to the pan, stir in the curry paste and cook very briefly. Tip in the tomatoes, then half-fill the empty can with water. Pour into the pan and stir in the pumpkin or squash.
2 Cover the pan and leave to simmer over a gentle heat for 20 minutes until the pumpkin or squash is tender. Add the chickpeas to heat through for 2–3 minutes, then season to taste. Serve with warmed naan bread.

• Per serving 317 kcalories, protein 30g, carbohydrate 20g, fat 14g, saturated fat 1g, fibre 5g, added sugar none, salt 1.12g

Thai red curry paste is a concentrated mixture of herbs and spices, flavoured with dried red chillies.

# Red pork curry with green beans

250g/9oz green beans, trimmed
1 tbsp vegetable oil
4 tsp Thai red curry paste
1 tbsp finely chopped ginger
500g/1lb 2oz pork fillet, thinly sliced
300ml/½ pint vegetable stock
2 tbsp fish sauce (nam pla)
1 tsp light muscovado sugar
400ml can coconut milk
400g can palm hearts, drained, rinsed and sliced
grated zest and juice of 1 large lime
a handful each of fresh basil and coriander leaves
rice noodles, to serve

Takes 30–40 minutes • Serves 4

1  Cook the beans in boiling salted water for 5 minutes, then drain and refresh under cold running water.
2  Heat the oil in a pan, add the curry paste and ginger, and fry gently until the oil separates out. Tip in the pork and stock, bring to the boil, then simmer for 5 minutes.
3  Add the fish sauce, sugar, coconut milk, palm hearts, lime zest and juice, and simmer for a further 5 minutes, adding the beans halfway through. Throw in the basil and coriander and serve with rice noodles.

• Per serving 396 kcalories, protein 32g, carbohydrate 10g, fat 26g, saturated fat 16g, fibre 2g, added sugar 1g, salt 2.29g

Creamy and mild, gently spiced coconut curries are always a popular choice on any menu.

# Prawn and coconut curry

4 tsp vegetable oil
1 tsp mustard seeds
1 small onion, finely chopped
1 tbsp finely chopped ginger
1 garlic clove, finely chopped
¼ tsp each ground turmeric and mild chilli powder
½ tsp ground coriander
2 fresh bay leaves
1 small green chilli, seeded and thinly sliced
10 raw king prawns, peeled
200ml carton coconut cream
1 lime, halved

Takes 30 minutes • Serves 2

1 Heat the oil in a frying pan. Fry the mustard seeds until they pop. Tip in the onion and fry, stirring, until golden. Add the ginger and garlic and cook for 1 minute, then add the turmeric, chilli powder and coriander and cook for 30 seconds more. Add the bay leaves and chilli, and cook for 1 minute.
2 Pour in 150ml/¼ pint water and bubble for a minute. Stir in the prawns. Lower the heat and simmer for 3–4 minutes, until the prawns are cooked.
3 Pour in the coconut cream, warm through, then squeeze in the juice from one of the lime halves. Season with salt and serve with the other lime half, cut into wedges.

• Per serving 519 kcalories, protein 23g, carbohydrate 12g, fat 42g, saturated fat 31g, fibre 1g, added sugar none, salt 3.08g

Use a good-quality, full-fat natural yogurt in this recipe or the sauce will split.

# Lamb korma with sultanas

250g/9oz Greek yogurt
2 tsp each ground cumin and coriander
¼ tsp cayenne pepper
4 tbsp chopped fresh coriander
5 tbsp sunflower or groundnut oil
5cm/2in piece of cinnamon stick
1 bay leaf
5 cardamom pods
900g/2lb boneless lamb shoulder, cut into chunky cubes
1 onion, finely chopped
50g/2oz sultanas
2 tbsp soured cream
naan bread, to serve

Takes 1½ hours • Serves 4–6

1  Mix the yogurt with the ground spices, chopped coriander, 1 teaspoon of salt and some freshly ground black pepper until smooth. Set aside.
2  Heat the oil in a wide pan and, when hot, add the cinnamon stick, bay leaf and cardamom pods. Cook the lamb in batches; adding as much as the pan will hold easily in a single layer. Brown well, remove, and repeat with the remaining lamb.
3  Add the onion to the pan and cook until browned, then return the meat to the pan with the yogurt mixture and sultanas.
4  Cover and simmer gently for 1 hour or until the lamb is tender. Uncover the pan and continue cooking until the sauce is thick. Stir in the soured cream and serve with naan.

• Per serving 808 kcalories, protein 46g, carbohydrate 15g, fat 63g, saturated fat 27g, fibre 1g, sugar 12g, salt 0.51g

If you like your curries fiery, this is the one for you.

# Vegetable vindaloo

1 tbsp sunflower oil
3 tbsp vindaloo curry paste
1 tbsp soft brown sugar
juice of ½ lemon
2 courgettes, thickly sliced
300g/10oz cauliflower florets (about
½ a head)
400ml/14fl oz passata
410g can chickpeas, drained
and rinsed
250g bag fresh leaf spinach, washed
basmati rice, to serve

Takes 35 minutes • Serves 4–6

1  Heat the oil in a large pan, add the curry paste and fry for 1 minute. Add the sugar and lemon juice, cook for 1 minute, then tip in the courgettes and cauliflower, and cook for 2 minutes. Now stir in the passata, plus 100ml/3½fl oz water and the chickpeas, season to taste. Bring to the boil, cover with a lid and simmer for 15 minutes.
2  Just before serving, throw in the spinach, give it a stir and remove from the heat once the leaves have just wilted. Serve with basmati rice.

• Per serving 142 kcalories, protein 8g, carbohydrate 16g, fat 6g, saturated fat none, fibre 4g, sugar 8g, salt 1.01g

This is the ultimate Thai classic; this recipe can be easily reproduced at home and is just as delicious as a good restaurant version.

# Thai green chicken curry

200g/8oz new potatoes, cut into chunks
100g/4oz green beans, trimmed and halved
1 tbsp sunflower oil
1 garlic clove, chopped
1 rounded tbsp Thai green curry paste
400ml can coconut milk
2 tsp Thai fish sauce (nam pla)
1 tsp caster sugar
450g/1lb skinless chicken breasts, cut into pieces
3 fresh kaffir lime leaves, finely shredded, or dried ones, crushed
a good handful of fresh basil leaves
rice, to serve

Takes 30–40 minutes • Serves 6

1  Boil the potatoes for 5 minutes, then throw in the beans and cook for a further 3 minutes, by which time both should be just tender. Drain away the water.
2  In a wok or large frying pan, heat the oil until very hot, then drop in the garlic and cook for a few seconds until golden. Add the curry paste for a few more seconds just to begin to cook the spices. Next, pour in the coconut milk and let it come to a bubble.
3  Stir in the fish sauce, sugar and chicken pieces. Simmer, covered, for about 8 minutes until the chicken is cooked.
4  Tip in the potatoes and beans, and warm through, then stir in most of the shredded or crushed lime leaves and the basil, and remove from the heat. Scatter with the remaining lime leaves and serve with rice.

• Per serving 245 kcalories, protein 20g, carbohydrate 10g, fat 14g, saturated fat 10g, fibre 1g, sugar 4g, salt 0.82g

Paneer is a firm low-fat Indian cheese. Lots of supermarkets sell it now, and you will find it in packets that are a bit like those for halloumi.

# Paneer masala

½ tsp cumin seeds
1 green chilli, seeded and chopped
½ × finger-length knob of ginger, chopped
150g/5oz Greek yogurt
1 tsp light muscovado sugar
½ tsp garam masala
2 tbsp chopped fresh coriander leaves and stems
juice of ½ lime
3 tbsp tomato purée
250g/9oz frozen peas
200g/8oz paneer, cut into 1cm cubes
2–3 tomatoes, cut into wedges
a handful of chopped roasted cashew nuts, to serve

Takes 35 minutes • Serves 2

1 Toast the cumin seeds in a heavy pan for about 30 seconds. Crush roughly in a pestle and mortar, then blitz until smooth in a blender with the chilli, ginger, yogurt, sugar, garam masala, coriander, lime juice, tomato purée and 200ml/7fl oz water.
2 Pour into a pan and cook for around 5 minutes, stirring. Add the peas for a further 3–5 minutes until almost cooked, then stir in the paneer and tomatoes, and heat through for 2–3 minutes. Serve scattered with cashew nuts.

• Per serving 607 kcalories, protein 44g, carbohydrate 24g, fat 38g, saturated fat 23g, fibre 8g, added sugar 3g, salt 3.26g

A real favourite from the takeaway menu – and a great mild choice for kids.

# Chicken korma

2 medium onions
4 tbsp sunflower oil
4 garlic cloves, crushed or finely chopped
1½ tsp garam masala
¼–½ tsp cayenne pepper
4 skinless chicken breast fillets, cut into chunks
500g pot natural yogurt
50g/2oz ground almonds
a handful of chopped fresh coriander
basmati rice, to serve

Takes 40 minutes • Serves 4

1  Finely chop one of the onions. Heat half the oil in a pan, add the chopped onion and garlic, and cook over a medium heat for 2–3 minutes. Add another tablespoon of oil, stir in the garam masala and cayenne, and continue to cook, stirring, for 1 minute.
2  Add the chicken and cook for a further 2–3 minutes. Stir in the yogurt and ground almonds, and simmer gently for 8–10 minutes or until the chicken is cooked.
3  Meanwhile, thinly slice the remaining onion and heat the remaining tablespoon of oil in a non-stick pan. Fry the onion until browned and crisp. Remove with a slotted spoon and drain on kitchen paper.
4  Stir the coriander and some seasoning into the curry and serve with some basmati rice, scattered with the crispy onions.

• Per serving 458 kcalories, protein 45g, carbohydrate 17g, fat 24g, saturated fat 5g, fibre 2g, sugar 14g, salt 0.48g

This is a delicious dish in its own right, but if there are any leftovers it makes a great topping for a jacket potato the next day.

# Vegetable balti

1 tbsp vegetable oil
1 large onion, thickly sliced
1 large garlic clove, crushed
1 eating apple, peeled, cored and chopped into chunks
3 tbsp balti curry paste
1 medium butternut squash, peeled and cut into chunks
2 large carrots, thickly sliced
200g/8oz turnips, cut into chunks
1 medium cauliflower, broken into florets
400g can chopped tomatoes
425ml/¾ pint hot vegetable stock
4 tbsp chopped fresh coriander, plus extra to sprinkle
150g pot natural yogurt
naan bread, to serve

Takes 1½ hours • Serves 4

1  Heat the oil in a very large pan, then add the onion, garlic and apple, and cook gently until softened. Stir in the curry paste.
2  Tip in all the vegetables, the chopped tomatoes and the stock with 3 tablespoons of coriander. Bring to the boil, then lower the heat, cover, and cook for 30 minutes. Uncover and cook for another 20 minutes until the vegetables are soft and the sauce thickened. Season.
3  Mix 1 tablespoon of coriander into the yogurt. Ladle the curry into warmed bowls and ripple some yogurt over the top. Sprinkle with extra chopped coriander, then serve with naan on the side.

• Per serving 201kcalories, protein 11g, carbohydrate 25g, fat 7g, saturated fat 1g, fibre 7g, added sugar none, salt 1.13g

This throw-it-together pilaf only takes 10 minutes,
perfect for an after-work supper.

# Tandoori chicken pilaf

1 tsp cumin seeds
400ml can reduced-fat coconut milk
1 chicken stock cube
400g/14oz cooked tandoori or
chicken tikka mini fillets
2 × 250g pouches cooked basmati
rice
200g/8oz baby leaf spinach
a handful of fresh coriander leaves
a handful of roasted salted
cashew nuts
poppadums and raita, to serve

Takes 10 minutes • Serves 4

1  Heat a large frying pan and dry-roast
the cumin seeds for 30 seconds. Add the
coconut milk and stock cube, and stir to
dissolve. Add the chicken, snipping each
piece into two or three as you drop them
in, if large. Cover and warm through for
around 2 minutes.
2  Add the rice, stirring to break up any
lumps, and pile the spinach on top with
3 tablespoons of water. Cover and cook
for 3–4 minutes until the spinach starts to wilt.
3  Tear the coriander and roughly chop
the nuts, and stir into the rice. Serve with
poppadums and raita.

• Per serving 805 kcalories, protein 42g, carbohydrate
102g, fat 27g, saturated fat 12g, fibre 2g, added sugar
none, salt 3.14g

This is a classic keema curry with a twist – there's no need for rice on the side, as we've turned this dish upside down and topped it with some spicy mash.

# Keema curry pies

1 large onion, chopped
2 tbsp sunflower oil
2 garlic cloves, crushed
a small knob of ginger, grated
2 tbsp medium curry powder
500g/1lb 2oz minced beef or lamb
400g can chopped tomatoes
100g/4oz frozen peas

FOR THE TOPPING
1kg/2lb 4oz mixed parsnips and
potatoes, peeled and cut
into chunks
1 green chilli, seeded and chopped
1 large bunch of fresh coriander,
chopped
2 tsp ground turmeric
juice of 1 lemon
50g/2oz butter

Takes 1½ hours • Serves 6

1  First, make the keema curry. Cook the onion in the oil until soft. Add the garlic, ginger and curry powder, and cook for 3 minutes, then increase the heat and add the mince. Fry until lightly browned, then add the tomatoes and simmer for around 20 minutes until thickened, throwing in the peas for the final minute.
2  Meanwhile, boil the parsnips and potatoes until tender. Drain, season and mash with the rest of the topping ingredients.
3  Preheat the oven to 220°C/200°C fan/ gas 7. Divide the keema curry among six small dishes, or spoon into one large one, and top with mash. Bake for 20 minutes until golden and bubbling.

• Per serving 424 kcalories, protein 22g, carbohydrate 27g, fat 26g, saturated fat 11g, fibre 8g, sugar 10g, salt 0.53g

Adding a little coconut cream at the end calms down the spiciness of this tasty Thai chicken dish.

# Thai yellow chicken with potatoes

1 tbsp vegetable oil
1 small onion, thinly sliced
400ml can coconut milk
200ml/7fl oz chicken stock
2 tbsp Thai yellow curry paste
3 tbsp fish sauce
2 tbsp sugar
750g/1lb 10oz potatoes, quartered and parboiled
4 skinless chicken breasts, sliced into 1cm-thick pieces
coconut cream, and a handful of chopped coriander, to garnish
steamed rice, to serve

Takes 40 minutes • Serves 4

1  In a large pan, heat the oil and cook the onion for 5–8 minutes until just golden.
2  Add the coconut milk, chicken stock and curry paste, and bring to the boil. Tip in the fish sauce and sugar; turn down to a simmer. Add the potatoes and chicken, then cook for 10 minutes or until the chicken and potatoes are cooked through. Season to taste.
3  Divide among four bowls, add a little coconut cream and a sprinkling of coriander to each. Serve with steamed rice.

• Per serving 537 kcalories, protein 41g, carbohydrate 45g, fat 22g, saturated fat 15g, fibre 3g, added sugar 8g, salt 3.19g

A biryani is a great all-in-one meal; just serve with raita,
if you like.

# Spiced vegetable biryani

2 tbsp vegetable oil
1 small cauliflower, broken
into small florets
2 large sweet potatoes, peeled
and cubed
1 large onion, sliced
1 litre/1¾ pints hot vegetable stock
3 tbsp hot curry paste (madras
is good)
1 red chilli, seeded and
finely chopped
½ tsp ground turmeric
2 tsp mustard seeds (black or white)
500g/1lb 2oz basmati rice
140g/5oz trimmed green beans,
halved
juice of 2 lemons
a handful of fresh coriander leaves
50g/2oz roasted salted
cashew nuts

Takes 1 hour • Serves 6

1  Preheat the oven to 220°C/200°C fan/
gas 7. Pour the oil into a large ovenproof dish
and heat in the oven for 5 minutes. Add the
vegetables, except the beans, stirring to coat
in the hot oil. Season and return to the oven
for 15 minutes until beginning to brown.
2  Meanwhile, in a bowl, stir together the
stock, curry paste, chilli, turmeric and
mustard seeds.
3  Mix the rice and green beans into the dish,
then pour over the stock mixture. Lower the
oven heat to 190°C/170°C fan/gas 5. Cover
the dish with foil and bake for 30 minutes
until the rice is tender and liquid absorbed.
Stir in the lemon juice, then scatter over the
coriander and cashews, and serve.

• Per serving 494 kcalories, protein 14g, carbohydrate
89g, fat 12g, saturated fat 1g, fibre 5g, added sugar
none, salt 0.99g

This chicken balti becomes a one-pan meal with the addition of some quinoa – if you don't fancy using quinoa, just swap it for basmati rice instead.

# Chicken balti one-pot

1 tbsp sunflower oil
2 large onions, thickly sliced
4 skinless chicken breasts
5 tbsp balti paste
200g/8oz quinoa
400g can chopped tomatoes
1 litre/1¾ pints chicken stock
50g/2oz roasted salted cashew nuts
1 small bunch of fresh coriander, leaves, chopped

Takes 35 minutes • Serves 4

1  Heat the oil in a large pan, fry the onions for 5 minutes until golden and softened, then tip on to a plate. Add the chicken breasts, browning for a few minutes on each side, then stir in the balti paste, quinoa and onions. Sizzle for a few minutes, then pour in the tomatoes and stock, and give everything a good mix. Bubble for 25 minutes until the quinoa is tender and saucy.
2  Stir in the cashews and most of the coriander with some seasoning, then scatter over the rest of the coriander to serve.

• Per serving 527 kcalories, protein 47g, carbohydrate 45g, fat 19g, saturated fat 3g, fibre 5g, sugar 14g, salt 1.83g

By cooking the rice separately, the pilaf has no chance of becoming too sticky.

# Spiced prawn and coconut pilaf

4 tbsp vegetable oil
1 tsp cumin seeds
1 cinnamon stick
3 each cloves and cardamom pods
1 onion, finely sliced
a fingertip-sized knob of ginger, roughly chopped
2 large garlic cloves, sliced
2 tomatoes, quartered
½ tsp ground turmeric
¼ tsp hot chilli powder
1 heaped tsp ground coriander
300g/10oz raw peeled prawns
250g/9oz basmati rice, cooked according to packet instructions
a handful of flaked coconut, to garnish (optional)

Takes 45 minutes • Serves 4

1  Heat the oil in a large non-stick pan, add the whole spices and, once they are sizzling, follow with the onion, frying for about 10 minutes until soft.

2  Meanwhile, make a paste using the ginger, garlic and tomatoes in a food processor. Add to the onion along with the remaining ground spices and cook over a low heat, stirring every now and then for 15 minutes.

3  Add the prawns and cook for a couple of minutes until pink. Stir in the cooked rice with a fork, heat through and serve scattered with the coconut, if using.

• Per serving 417 kcalories, protein 19g, carbohydrate 60g, fat 13g, saturated fat 2g, fibre 1g, sugar 3g, salt 0.42g

Serve with basmati rice cooked with cardamom pods,
cloves and a cinnamon stick.

# Chilli chicken curry

1 medium onion, roughly chopped
½ × finger-length knob ginger,
roughly chopped
2 garlic cloves, roughly chopped
1 tsp cumin seeds
2 tbsp vegetable oil
½ tsp each ground turmeric and hot
chilli powder
½ × 400g can chopped tomatoes
350g/12oz potatoes, peeled and cut
into chunks
500g/1lb 2oz skinless chicken
breasts, cut into chunks
½ tsp garam masala
2 tbsp chopped fresh coriander,
to garnish
cooked flavoured rice (see intro
above) and natural yogurt,
to serve

Takes 1 hour • Serves 4

1 Blitz the onion, ginger and garlic in a
food processor with 1 tablespoon water
until smooth.
2 Fry the cumin seeds in the oil for a few
seconds, then add the onion paste to soften
for 5 minutes – splashing in a little water if it
starts to catch. Sprinkle in the turmeric and
chilli. Add the tomatoes and fry for 5 minutes.
Stir in the potatoes and 225ml/8fl oz hot
water. Cook, covered, for 10 minutes.
3 Add the chicken and garam masala.
Simmer for 15–20 minutes until cooked.
Season, scatter over the coriander and serve
with rice and natural yogurt.

• Per serving 283 kcalories, protein 34g, carbohydrate
21g, fat 8g, saturated fat 1g, fibre 2g, added sugar
none, salt 0.35g

If you can, make this the day before and reheat to serve
– the flavours will be even better.

# Kashmiri lamb with tomatoes and aromatic spices

1 tbsp vegetable oil
1 tsp each cumin seeds and whole cloves
1 cinnamon stick, broken in half
4 bay leaves
2 medium onions, sliced
800g/1lb 12oz lean boneless lamb leg, cut into chunks
2 garlic cloves, crushed
½ × finger-length knob ginger, cut into matchsticks
1 tbsp ground coriander
½ tsp each cayenne pepper and ground turmeric
2 medium potatoes, peeled and each cut into 4–6 chunks
400g can chopped tomatoes
150g pot natural yogurt and 2 tbsp chopped fresh coriander, to serve

Takes 2 hours • Serves 6

1 Heat the oil in a large pan. Sprinkle in the cumin seeds and, when crackling, throw in the cloves, cinnamon and bay leaves for 30 seconds. Add the onions for 10 minutes to soften, then the lamb, frying for around 12–15 minutes until browned.

2 Stir in the garlic, ginger, ground spices, potatoes and 1 teaspoon salt for roughly 2–3 minutes. Add the tomatoes and 300ml/½ pint hot water just to cover. Bring to the boil, then reduce the heat, cover and simmer gently for 1 hour or until the lamb is tender. Swirl in the yogurt and coriander, to garnish, then serve.

• Per serving 290 kcalories, protein 29g, carbohydrate 11g, fat 14g, saturated fat 5g, fibre 2g, added sugar none, salt 0.4g

For a Thai-themed evening, serve this dish alongside a creamy green chicken curry (as on page 134), a mound of jasmine rice and a crunchy Thai-style salad (like the one on page 150).

# Red prawns with chilli and lime leaf

3 long dried red chillies, seeded and roughly chopped
½ tsp each coriander and cumin seeds
4 garlic cloves, finely chopped
1 lemongrass stalk, chopped
2 tbsp chopped coriander stalks
6 kaffir lime leaves, 3 finely shredded
a fingertip-sized knob ginger, chopped
2 tsp shrimp paste
3 tbsp oil
400g/14oz large raw peeled prawns, de-veined
1½ tbsp each Thai fish sauce, caster sugar and fresh lemon juice

Takes 20 minutes • Serves 6

1  To make the red curry paste, put the dried chillies, coriander and cumin seeds, 1 teaspoon chopped garlic, lemongrass, coriander stalks, whole lime leaves, ginger and shrimp paste into a food processor, and whiz to a paste.
2  In a wok or frying pan, heat the oil and fry the remaining garlic until golden. Stir in the red curry paste and cook together for a few seconds. Add 3 tablespoons water and mix thoroughly. Tip in the prawns and cook for a few seconds over a high heat until evenly pink.
3  Stirring quickly after each addition, add the fish sauce, sugar, lemon juice and shredded lime leaves. Stir thoroughly for 2–3 seconds then serve.

• Per serving 146 kcalories, protein 13g, carbohydrate 6g, fat 8g, saturated fat 1g, fibre 0.1g, sugar 4g, salt 1.41g

Sit this warming pot in the middle of the table and let everyone help themselves.

# Spicy lamb and squash supper

2 tbsp sunflower oil
1 onion, chopped
450g/1lb lamb fillet, cut into small pieces
1 garlic clove, chopped
2 tsp each ground cumin, ground coriander and hot chilli powder
1 small butternut squash, peeled and cut into small chunks
400g can chopped tomatoes
850ml/1½ pints lamb stock
50g/2oz red lentils
3 tbsp chopped fresh coriander

Takes 1 hour • Serves 4

1 Heat the oil in a large pan and fry the onion for about 4 minutes until golden. Stir in the lamb and garlic, and fry over a high heat for 3–4 minutes, stirring, until the lamb starts to brown. Add the spices and cook for 30 seconds, stirring constantly. Stir in the squash chunks.

2 Pour in the tomatoes and stock, add the lentils and bring to the boil. Simmer, partially covered, for about 30 minutes until the lamb and squash are tender. Season and stir in the coriander just before serving, reserving a little to sprinkle over the top.

• Per serving 459 kcalories, protein 26g, carbohydrate 31g, fat 27g, saturated fat 11g, fibre 4g, added sugar none, salt 1g

Tamarind is a sweet–sour paste often used in Indian cooking – you'll find it in small jars near the spices in the supermarket.

# Tamarind fish curry

700g/1lb 9oz white fish fillet, skinned and cut into chunks
2 tbsp tamarind paste
2 tbsp vegetable oil
1 tsp mustard seeds
1 small onion, chopped
2 tbsp chopped ginger
2 plump garlic cloves, finely chopped
½ tsp ground turmeric
8 curry leaves (optional)
2 small green chillies, seeded and thinly sliced
1 tsp ground coriander
¼ tsp ground cinnamon
150ml/¼ pint coconut milk
1 tsp malt vinegar
rice, to serve

Takes 45 minutes • Serves 6

1  Pat dry the fish with kitchen paper. Dissolve the tamarind paste in a shallow bowl of 150ml/¼ pint water, then add the fish to it for 15 minutes.

2  Meanwhile, heat the oil in a wok or frying pan. Fry the mustard seeds until crackling then stir in the onion and fry until brown. Add the ginger and garlic, and cook for 2 minutes, then the turmeric, curry leaves (if using), chillies, coriander and cinnamon, and stir for 1–2 minutes more. Add the coconut milk for 3–4 minutes.

3  Lift the fish out of the tamarind water, then add the water and the vinegar to the wok or pan and bring to the boil. Put in the fish, lower the heat and simmer for 5 minutes until the fish is just cooked. Serve with rice.

• Per serving 196 kcalories, protein 23g, carbohydrate 6g, fat 9g, saturated fat 4g, fibre 0.2g, sugar 5g, salt 0.27g

In Goan cuisine, vinegar is often mixed with spices, giving a hot sharpness that cuts through rich meats such as pork belly.

# Goan pork curry

1.8kg/4lb pork belly, skinned and cut into large cubes
200ml/7fl oz white wine vinegar
1 tbsp hot chilli powder
3 tsp ground turmeric
2 tsp yellow mustard seeds
4 tsp cumin seeds
sunflower oil, for frying
7 onions, 6 chopped and 1 sliced
8 garlic cloves, crushed
a thumb-sized knob ginger, grated
chutney and naan bread, to serve

Takes 2½ hours, plus marinating • Serves 8

1  Put the meat in a large non-metallic bowl with the vinegar and spices. Mix well, cover and chill for up to 24 hours.
2  Heat 3 tablespoons oil in a deep frying pan, then fry the chopped onions, garlic and ginger for 10 minutes until softened. Tip in the meat and all of the marinade, season, then let the meat cook in its own juices for about 10 minutes – it doesn't need to brown. Pour in enough water to cover, then simmer for about 1½ hours until the meat is very tender.
3  Meanwhile, heat 1cm oil in a frying pan until hot, then fry the sliced onion for 4 minutes or until crisp and golden. Drain on kitchen paper, then sprinkle over the curry to serve, along with chutney and naan.

• Per serving 695 kcalories, protein 46g, carbohydrate 13g, fat 51g, saturated fat 19g, fibre 2g, sugar 6g, salt 0.51g

Serve this aromatic, creamy curry with a colourful
Thai salad on the side.

# Chicken with lemongrass and coconut

2 × 400ml cans coconut milk
3 tbsp fish sauce
½ × finger-length knob of ginger or
galangal, finely chopped
2 lemongrass stalks, finely sliced
6 dried kaffir lime leaves
1 fresh red chilli, seeded
and chopped
2 tsp light muscovado sugar
500g/1lb 2oz skinless chicken
breasts, cut in chunks
2 tbsp fresh lime juice
a good handful of fresh basil and
coriander, roughly chopped,
to garnish
steamed Thai jasmine rice, to serve

Takes 40 minutes • Serves 4, or 6 with
other dishes

1 Tip all the ingredients except the chicken,
lime juice and herbs into a pan, bring to a
gentle simmer and cook uncovered at a
relaxed bubble for 5 minutes.
2 Add the chicken and cover and simmer
for 15 minutes until the chicken is tender. Stir
in the lime juice, then scatter over the herbs
before serving with Thai jasmine rice.

• Per serving (4) 454 kcalories, protein 26g,
carbohydrate 39g, fat 23g, saturated fat 19g,
fibre 1g, added sugar 2g, salt 1.89g

In India saffron is known as the royal spice and adds a sense of celebration and indulgence to food, which makes this dish ideal for serving at Diwali.

# Saffron-scented chicken

1 tbsp vegetable oil
1 tsp fennel seeds
2 garlic cloves, finely sliced
2 small onions, finely chopped
6 skinless chicken breasts, each halved diagonally
4 tbsp korma curry paste
a few saffron strands, plus extra to serve
6 tbsp double cream
150g pot natural yogurt
1½ tsp clear honey
a handful of sliced toasted almonds and hot naan bread, to serve

Takes 50 minutes • Serves 6

1  Heat the oil in a pan and add the fennel seeds. When they begin to sizzle, add the garlic and onions. Sprinkle in some water, then cook for 5–8 minutes, or until golden.
2  Add the chicken to the pan and seal quickly. Add the korma paste and stir for 2 minutes. Add the saffron and 200ml/7fl oz water, cover, then simmer for 10–15 minutes to cook the chicken through completely.
3  Stir in the cream, yogurt and honey, and leave to cook for 3–5 minutes more. Serve topped with almonds, a few extra strands of saffron and some hot naan bread.

• Per serving 269 kcalories, protein 34g, carbohydrate 5g, fat 13g, saturated fat 5g, fibre none, sugar 4g, salt 0.64g

The korma paste used in this biryani adds its flavours of coconut, ginger, coriander and turmeric to the dish.

# Fragrant vegetable and cashew biryani

8 tbsp sunflower oil
4 onions, halved and thinly sliced
a thumb-sized knob of ginger, shredded
5 tbsp korma curry paste
2 cinnamon sticks
6 green cardamom pods
3 star anise
800g/1lb 12oz mix diced potato, cauliflower florets and frozen peas
250g/9oz Greek yogurt
½ tsp each rosewater and ground turmeric
500g pack basmati rice, covered with water and soaked for 30 minutes
100g/4oz roasted salted cashew nuts
a handful of fresh coriander leaves

Takes 2 hours • Serves 8

1  First, heat 4 tablespoons of the oil and soften half of the onions. Add the ginger, curry paste, whole spices, potato and cauliflower for 1 minute, then add 300ml/½ pint water, cover and cook for 6 minutes. Stir in the peas, yogurt and 1 teaspoon salt.
2  In a bowl, mix together the rosewater, turmeric and 3 tablespoons water. Drain the rice, boil in a pan of water for 5 minutes, then drain again.
3  Preheat the oven to 180°C/160°C fan/gas 4. Oil a large ovenproof dish with a lid. Layer in the sauce, nuts and rice, then drizzle over the rosewater mix. Cover with foil first, then the lid, and bake for 45 minutes–1 hour until hot through. To garnish, fry the remaining onions in the rest of the oil and add to the biryani with the coriander.

• Per serving 469 kcalories, protein 14g, carbohydrate 67g, fat 18g, saturated fat 4g, fibre 4g, sugar 7g, salt 1.11g

Serve this delicious dish with warm naans to mop up the sauce. If you buy mini naans you can pop them in the toaster to heat, freeing up your oven if you're entertaining.

# Spicy lamb

a thumb-sized knob of ginger, roughly chopped
2 onions, quartered
8 garlic cloves
2 mild red chillies, trimmed (and seeded if you like a milder flavour)
1 large bunch of fresh coriander
2 tbsp each fennel seeds, ground coriander and ground cumin
1.6kg/3lb 8oz diced lamb leg
2 tbsp olive oil
2 × 400g cans chopped tomatoes
2 tbsp tomato purée
300ml/½ pint lamb or vegetable stock
200g/8oz frozen peas
a handful of chopped fresh mint

Takes 2 hours 20 minutes • Serves 8

1  Put the ginger, onions, garlic, chillies and two-thirds of the coriander into a food processor and whiz to a coarse paste. Toss the fennel seeds, ground coriander and cumin with the lamb to coat.
2  Heat the oil in a large heavy-based pan and fry the lamb in batches for 4–5 minutes until well browned. Return all the meat to the pan, stir in the paste and fry for 8–10 minutes, stirring occasionally. Add the tomatoes, tomato purée and stock. Bring to the boil, cover and simmer gently for 1½ hours until the meat is tender.
3  Stir in the peas and seasoning, and simmer gently for 3–4 minutes. Chop the remaining coriander and mint, and scatter over to serve.

• Per serving 485 kcalories, protein 44g, carbohydrate 12g, fat 30g, saturated fat 13g, fibre 3g, sugar 5g, salt 0.67g

For something different, try this Caribbean curry. Serve with coconut rice, buttered corn cobs and lime wedges.

# Jerk chicken curry with beans

8 chicken drumsticks or thighs
2 tbsp jerk seasoning
4 tsp olive oil
2 red onions, sliced
1 small bunch of fresh coriander, stalks finely chopped, leaves reserved
2 × 400g cans chopped tomatoes
410g can kidney beans, drained and rinsed

Takes 50 minutes • Serves 4

1  Toss the chicken in half the jerk seasoning and a little salt and pepper. Heat half the oil in a large frying pan, quickly brown the chicken, then remove. Tip in the remaining oil, onions and coriander stalks, then soften for 5 minutes, stirring in the remaining jerk seasoning for the final minute.

2  Return the drumsticks or thighs to the pan, pour over the tomatoes, then bring to a simmer. Cover, then cook for 30 minutes. Remove the lid, stir in the beans, then cook for a further 10–15 minutes until the chicken is tender. Scatter with the coriander leaves and serve.

• Per serving 438 kcalories, protein 45g, carbohydrate 23g, fat 19g, saturated fat 5g, fibre 7g, sugar 9g, salt 1.68g

This colourful one-pan dish is made for entertaining
– try it with beef too.

# Lamb, coconut and mango pilaf

1 tbsp sunflower oil
600g/1lb 5oz lamb shoulder, cut into large cubes
2 onions, sliced
2 garlic cloves, sliced
3 tbsp medium curry powder
1 fat red chilli, seeded and thickly sliced
400ml can reduced-fat coconut milk
700ml/1¼ pints hot lamb stock
400g/14oz basmati rice
1 medium mango, peeled, stoned and sliced, plus a handful each of chopped fresh coriander and toasted flaked almonds, to garnish
poppadoms, to serve

Takes 2 hours • Serves 6

1  Preheat the oven to 180°C/160°C fan/gas 4. Heat the oil in a large, shallow ovenproof pan, tip in the lamb, then fry for 5 minutes until browned all over. Remove from the pan and set aside. Add the onions to the pan and fry until soft and golden. Tip in the garlic and curry powder, and fry for 1 minute more.
2  Stir the lamb back in with the chilli, coconut milk and stock, then bring to the boil. Cover and bake for 1 hour, until the lamb is tender.
3  Season, stir in the rice, re-cover pan, then return to oven for 30 minutes until liquid has been absorbed. Stand, covered, for 10 minutes, then fluff the rice with a fork. Scatter with the sliced mango, coriander and almonds, then serve straight from the pan with some poppadoms, if you like.

• Per serving 575 kcalories, protein 27g, carbohydrate 67g, fat 24g, saturated fat 13g, fibre 4g, added sugar none, salt 0.82g

Chicken thighs have a wonderful flavour when slow cooked.

# Cumin-spiced chicken with tomatoes

4 tsp cumin seeds
3 tbsp vegetable oil
2 onions, diced
700g/1lb 9oz skinless chicken thighs
3 garlic cloves, chopped
½ × finger-length knob of ginger, cut into thin sticks
400g can chopped tomatoes
¼ tsp ground turmeric
½ tsp chilli powder
2 tsp garam masala
3 tbsp chopped fresh coriander leaves

Takes 1¼ hours • Serves 4

1 Dry-roast 2 teaspoons of the cumin seeds in a pan for a few minutes. Set aside.
2 Heat the oil in a wok or frying pan and add the remaining cumin seeds. When crackling, add the onions and fry until softened. Add the chicken for 5 minutes to seal, then add the garlic and ginger for 3–4 minutes more. Stir in the tomatoes, turmeric, chilli, garam masala, 2 tablespoons of the coriander leaves and 1 teaspoon salt, then cover and simmer for 45 minutes until the chicken is tender and the sauce is thick – if it is too runny, remove the lid and cook to reduce.
3 Coarsely grind the roasted cumin seeds and sprinkle over the dish with the remaining coriander leaves. Remove from the heat and cover for 5 minutes before serving.

• Per serving 320 kcalories, protein 36g, carbohydrate 12g, fat 14g, saturated fat 3g, fibre 2g, added sugar none, salt 1.86g

When served together chickpeas and rice have the same nutritional value as protein in meat, making this a good curry for vegetarians.

# Vegetable curry with tamarind

1 tsp each cumin and coriander seeds
1 dried red chilli
1 tbsp vegetable oil
½ × thumb-sized knob of ginger, grated
2 garlic cloves, finely chopped
1 large potato and 2 carrots, cut into small chunks
200g pot Greek yogurt
1 tsp each ground turmeric and chilli powder
1–2 tbsp tamarind paste
1 cinnamon stick
½ cauliflower, broken into florets
140g/5oz frozen peas or green beans
410g can chickpeas, drained and rinsed
a handful of coriander leaves

Takes 1 hour 40 minutes • Serves 4

1  Dry-fry the cumin, coriander and chilli until fragrant. Add the oil, ginger and garlic, and fry until softened. Stir in the potato, carrots, yogurt, turmeric and chilli powder, then add 700ml/1¼ pints water, the tamarind paste, cinnamon and some seasoning. Bring to the boil, then lower the heat, cover, and simmer for 20 minutes, stirring occasionally.
2  Add the cauliflower for 10 minutes, then add the peas or beans and chickpeas for 10 minutes more and serve.

• Per serving 290 kcalories, protein 15g, carbohydrate 34g, fat 11g, saturated fat 4g, fibre 7g, added sugar none, salt 1.88g

The leftover paste can be frozen for 3 months – add it to any recipe that calls for Thai green curry paste – or if time is short you can just use a bought jar.

# Green chicken curry with aubergine

6 kaffir lime leaves, 3 finely shredded
1 tbsp each vegetable oil
400ml can coconut milk
1 tbsp Thai fish sauce
1 tsp each caster sugar and lime juice
450g/1lb skinless chicken breast, cut into bite-sized pieces
1 large or 6 baby aubergines, cut into chunks
15 Thai basil leaves (optional)

FOR THE GREEN CURRY PASTE
3 green chillies, trimmed
1 lemongrass stick
3 shallots, roughly chopped
3 garlic cloves
½ × finger-length knob of ginger, chopped
3 tbsp chopped fresh coriander roots or stalks
1 tsp each ground coriander, ground cumin and shrimp paste

Takes 25 minutes • Serves 6

1  Put all the paste ingredients plus the whole lime leaves in a food processor and whiz to a paste.

2  In a wok or a large frying pan, heat the oil until very hot, then add 3 tablespoons of the curry paste and fry for a few seconds. Pour in the coconut milk, 100ml/3½fl oz water, fish sauce, sugar and lime juice, cover and simmer for 10 minutes. Then add the chicken and aubergines, and simmer gently for 8 minutes until both cooked through. Stir in salt to taste, the shredded lime leaves and basil leaves, if using, and serve.

• Per serving 236 kcalories, protein 21g, carbohydrate 6g, fat 15g, saturated fat 10g, fibre 1g, sugar 4g, salt 0.97g

Easy but impressive looking, serve as one of a selection of dishes.

# Golden coconut curry with prawns

2 onions, sliced
a thumb-sized knob of ginger, grated
4 garlic cloves, crushed
2 tbsp sunflower oil
½ tsp ground turmeric
1 tbsp ground coriander
400g can chopped tomatoes
100g/4oz creamed coconut, chopped
1 tbsp mango chutney
1 green chilli, halved, seeded and sliced
1 large green pepper, quartered, seeded and sliced
600g/1lb 5oz large raw peeled prawns
a handful of chopped fresh coriander
juice of 1 lemon

Takes 35 minutes • Serves 8, with other dishes

1  Fry the onions, ginger and garlic in the oil for about 10 minutes. Stir in the turmeric and ground coriander, then fry for 1 minute more. Tip the mixture into a blender with the tomatoes and creamed coconut, then blend to a purée.

2  Return to the pan with 300ml/½ pint water, the chutney, chilli and pepper and simmer for 10 minutes.

3  Stir in the prawns and cook for a few minutes more, just until they turn pink. Add the chopped coriander, then season to taste with salt, pepper and a little lemon juice just before serving.

• Per serving 163 kcalories, protein 15g, carbohydrate 8g, fat 8g, saturated fat 4g, fibre 1g, sugar 5g, salt 0.55g

If you're making this for vegetarians, leave out the fish sauce and splash in a little soy sauce instead.

# Aubergine curry with lemongrass and coconut milk

3 large red chillies, seeded and chopped
6 garlic cloves, roughly chopped
a knob of ginger, chopped
2 lemongrass stalks, chopped
2 tbsp ground turmeric
1 tsp chilli powder
3 aubergines, quartered lengthways, then halved
1 tbsp olive oil
1 tbsp sugar
6 shallots, finely chopped
1 tbsp Thai fish sauce
400ml can coconut milk
400ml/14fl oz vegetable stock
1 small bunch of fresh coriander, roughly chopped, to garnish
jasmine rice or naan bread, to serve

Takes 40 minutes • Serves 4

1  In a food processor, pulse the chillies, garlic, ginger and lemongrass to a paste. Mix the turmeric and chilli powder together and rub all over the aubergine wedges.
2  Heat the oil in a frying pan, brown the aubergines, then remove and set aside. Cook the paste, sugar and shallots for a few minutes, then return the aubergines to the pan. Add the fish sauce, coconut milk and stock, and bring to the boil. Reduce the heat and cook gently until aubergine is tender, but not mushy, about 15 minutes. Season, sprinkle with the coriander and serve with steamed rice or warm naan bread to mop up the sauce.

• Per serving 268 kcalories, protein 5g, carbohydrate 17g, fat 20g, saturated fat 14g, fibre 3g, sugar 10g, salt 1.39g

This is a light curry that provides balance alongside richer dishes.

# Black pepper chicken

175gl/6oz natural yogurt
1 small bunch of fresh coriander,
leaves chopped
2 tbsp peppercorns, coarsely
crushed
2 tbsp grated ginger
2 tbsp crushed garlic
1 tbsp fresh lemon juice
900g/2lb skinless chicken breasts,
cut into large chunks
4 tbsp vegetable oil
1 large onion, chopped
1 tsp garam masala
1 large tomato, chopped

Takes 1 hour, plus marinating
Serves 6

1  In a bowl, mix together the yogurt, coriander, peppercorns, half the ginger, half the garlic, the lemon juice and some salt. Stir in the chicken and leave to marinate for 1 hour.
2  Heat the oil in a wok or a wide pan, then fry the onion until browned. Stir in the masala, remaining ginger and garlic and the chopped tomato, then reduce the heat and cook for 10–15 minutes, uncovered, stirring occasionally.
3  Add the chicken and marinade to the pan. Pour in 75–100ml/2½–3½fl oz water, or enough to make a thickish sauce. Bring to the boil, cover and simmer gently for 25 minutes, stirring occasionally, until the chicken is cooked through.

• Per serving 175 kcalories, protein 39g, carbohydrate 10g, fat 10g, saturated fat 2g, fibre 1g, sugar 5g, salt 0.3g

OK, so it isn't authentic, but a fragrant mash is ideal
for mopping up curry sauces.

# Lamb, chickpea and spinach curry with masala mash

1 tbsp oil
500g/1lb 2oz lean lamb leg, cubed
1 red onion, sliced
a fingertip-sized knob of ginger,
finely chopped
2 garlic cloves, crushed
1 tbsp each ground cumin and
ground coriander
400g can chopped tomatoes
½ × 410g can chickpeas, drained
and rinsed
1 tsp garam masala
100g/4oz fresh spinach, roughly
chopped
700g/1lb 9oz potatoes, peeled
and quartered
1 tbsp korma curry paste
100g/3½oz thick yogurt

Takes 1¾ hours • Serves 4

1  Heat the oil in a large frying pan, brown the lamb thoroughly then remove. Add the onion and cook until golden brown, then stir in the ginger, garlic, cumin and coriander, and cook for 2 minutes more until fragrant. Return the lamb to the pan, add the tomatoes, bring to the boil, then simmer gently for 1½ hours until the meat is really tender. (Add splashes of water if the sauce becomes too dry.) Add the chickpeas and garam masala then simmer for 5 minutes more. Stir through the spinach to wilt, then season.
2  Meanwhile, boil the potatoes until soft, about 15 minutes. Drain and mash with the curry paste and yogurt. Serve with the curry.

• Per serving 469 kcalories, protein 38g, carbohydrate 48g, fat 15g, saturated fat 5g, fibre 6g, added sugar none, salt 1.04g

This is a delicious curry by itself, or served as an accompaniment to a spicy roasted chicken or leg of lamb.

# Pumpkin curry with chickpeas

1 tbsp sunflower oil
3 tbsp Thai yellow curry paste
2 onions, finely chopped
3 large lemongrass sticks, bashed
6 cardamom pods
1 tbsp mustard seeds
1kg/2lb 4oz butternut squash, peeled, seeded and cut into chunks
400ml/14fl oz vegetable stock
400ml can reduced-fat coconut milk
410g can chickpeas, drained and rinsed
2 limes
a large handful of fresh mint leaves, to garnish
naan bread, to serve

1 Heat the oil in a deep frying pan, then gently fry the paste, onions, lemongrass, cardamom pods and mustard seeds for 2–3 minutes until fragrant. Stir in the squash for a few minutes, then pour in the stock and coconut milk. Bring to a simmer and cook for 20 minutes, then add the chickpeas for another 10 minutes until the squash is tender.
2 Squeeze the juice of one lime into the curry, then cut the other into wedges. Tear over the mint leaves, then serve with lime wedges and naan bread.

• Per serving 293 kcalories, protein 9g, carbohydrate 26g, fat 18g, saturated fat 10g, fibre 7g, sugar 10g, salt 1.3g

Takes 40 minutes • Serves 4

Keep dinner guests happy nibbling on these while you
finish preparing the main course.

# Coriander, tomato and mango dips with poppadums

**FOR THE CREAMY CORIANDER**
½ × thumb-sized knob of ginger,
roughly chopped
2 garlic cloves
½ small bunch of fresh coriander,
leaves only
½ mild red chilli, seeded and
finely chopped
300g/10oz natural yogurt

**FOR THE CHUNKY TOMATO**
4 tomatoes, finely chopped
1 small red onion, finely chopped
2 tsp kalonji seeds (also known as
black onion or nigella seeds)
juice of 1 lime
1 tbsp chopped fresh coriander

a small jar of mango chutney and
8 poppadums, to serve

Takes 30 minutes • Serves 8

1  For the creamy coriander dip, whiz the ginger, garlic, coriander and most of the chilli to a paste in a food processor. Stir with the yogurt and chill until ready to serve.
2  For the tomato dip, combine the chopped tomatoes, onion, kalonji seeds, lime juice and coriander with some seasoning, and set aside for the time being.
3  To serve, scatter the coriander dip with remaining chilli, scrape the mango chutney into a bowl, and transfer the chunky tomato to a serving bowl. Eat with poppadums.

• Per serving (mango chutney and poppadums not included) 46 kcalories, protein 3g, carbohydrate 6g, fat 2g, saturated fat 1g, fibre 1g, sugar 5g, salt 0.09g

This golden rice will work with almost any Indian curry.

# Spicy Indian rice

2 onions, sliced
2 tbsp sunflower oil
½ tsp ground turmeric
1 cinnamon stick
a mugful of long grain rice
6 cardamom pods, bashed with a
rolling pin
1 tsp cumin seeds
a large handful of sultanas
a large handful of roasted
cashew nuts

Takes 30 minutes • Serves 4

1 Fry the onions in the oil in a large frying pan for 10–12 minutes until golden. Set aside.
2 Fill a big pan with water, bring to the boil and tip in a heaped teaspoon of salt – the water will bubble furiously. Add the turmeric, cinnamon stick and rice. Stir once and return to the boil, then turn the heat down a little so that the water is boiling steadily, but not vigorously. Boil uncovered, without stirring, for 10 minutes until the rice is tender but with a little bite. Drain in a large sieve and rinse by pouring over a kettle of boiling water.
3 Stir the cardamom pods into the pan of onions with the cumin seeds, return to the heat and fry briefly. Toss in the sultanas and roasted cashew nuts, then the hot drained rice. Serve immediately.

• Per serving 449 kcalories, protein 8g, carbohydrate 82g, fat 12g, saturated fat 2g, fibre 1g, sugar 13g, salt 0.03g

A sharp, fresh salad – ideal for serving alongside creamy Thai curries.

# Thai cucumber salad with sour chilli dressing

1 cucumber, cut into ribbons with a peeler
1 Little Gem lettuce, shredded
140g/5oz beansprouts
1 bunch of fresh coriander, leaves roughly chopped
1 bunch of fresh mint, leaves roughly chopped

FOR THE DRESSING
1 tsp rice wine vinegar
1 tbsp fish sauce
½ tsp light muscovado sugar
2 red chillies, seeded and finely chopped

Takes 10 minutes • Serves 4

1  Mix the dressing ingredients together, stirring until the sugar is dissolved, then set aside until ready to serve.
2  Place the salad ingredients in a bowl, then pour over the dressing, mixing well to combine. Serve immediately.

• Per serving 27 kcalories, protein 2g, carbohydrate 4g, fat 1g, saturated fat none, fibre 1g, sugar 3g, salt 0.75g

Jaipur is the capital of Rajasthan, where the food tends to be milder and subtly spiced.

# Vegetables with Jaipuri spices

2 tbsp vegetable oil
1 tsp cumin seeds
2 small onions, chopped
2 tbsp rogan josh curry paste
200g/8oz potatoes, peeled and diced
5 tomatoes, roughly chopped
2 large carrots, peeled, halved and sliced lengthways
200g/8oz green beans, trimmed
200g/8oz peas, thawed if frozen
4 tbsp Greek yogurt
3 tbsp chopped fresh coriander
juice of ½ lemon

Takes 1 hour • Serves 6

1  Heat the oil in a pan, then add the cumin seeds. When they sizzle, add the onions and cook for 5–8 minutes or until golden brown. Stir in the curry paste and 50ml/2fl oz water, then cook for 2 more minutes.
2  Mix in the potatoes, stir well, then tip in the tomatoes and 225ml/8fl oz water. Cover and cook for 10 minutes before adding the carrots for another 10 minutes. Stir occasionally to prevent the sauce sticking. Add the green beans for around 5 minutes more, then the peas, Greek yogurt and 2 tablespoons of the coriander. Leave to cook for 2 more minutes before checking the seasoning. Squeeze in the lemon juice and serve garnished with the remaining coriander.

• Per serving 138 kcalories, protein 5g, carbohydrate 14g, fat 8g, saturated fat 2g, fibre 4g, sugar 7g, salt 0.31g

These spicy spuds are quick to prepare and make a nice change from Bombay potatoes.

# Chilli-roasted new potatoes

700g/1lb 9oz baby new potatoes
2 tbsp olive oil
2 tbsp tomato purée
2 garlic cloves, finely chopped
1 tsp chilli powder
flaked sea salt, to serve

Takes 55 minutes • Serves 4

1 Preheat the oven to 200°C/180°C fan/gas 6. Tip the potatoes into a roasting tin. Mix together the oil, tomato purée, garlic and chilli powder. Season with some freshly ground black pepper then mix with the potatoes until they are completely coated.

2 Transfer to the oven and roast, turning occasionally, for about 50 minutes until the potatoes are cooked and their skins are crisp. Sprinkle with sea salt and serve immediately.

• Per serving 184 kcalories, protein 4g, carbohydrate 30g, fat 6g, saturated fat 1g, fibre 2g, added sugar none, salt 0.13g

This sweet–sour relish makes a great accompaniment to some warm naan or a spicy curry.

# Fresh mango relish

2 large ripe mangoes
juice of 1 lime
1 tbsp tamarind paste
a handful each of fresh mint and
coriander leaves

Takes 15 minutes • Serves 4–6

1  Peel and stone both mangoes then finely dice two-thirds of the flesh. Tip into a small serving bowl.

2  Roughly chop the remaining flesh and put in a small food processor or blender with the lime juice and tamarind paste. Whiz until smooth, then add the herbs and pulse for a second. Stir the mango sauce into the diced mango and chill for up to an hour before serving.

• Per serving 68 kcalories, protein 1g, carbohydrate 17g, fat trace, saturated fat none, fibre 3g, added sugar none, salt 0.01g

Colourful and crunchy, this salad works well as part of a large spread and can be easily doubled to feed a crowd.

# Tomato, cucumber and coriander salad

6 vine tomatoes, chopped
1 small cucumber, diced
1 red onion, finely chopped
2 tbsp chopped fresh coriander

Takes 15 minutes • Serves 6

1  Mix together all of the salad ingredients and chill.
2  About 15 minutes before you are ready to eat, remove the salad from the fridge and let it come to room temperature. Season just before serving (otherwise the salad can become watery).

• Per serving 34 kcalories, protein 2g, carbohydrate 6g, fat none, saturated fat none, fibre 2g, sugar 6g, salt 0.03g

A good midweek accompaniment to a quick Thai curry; you get your noodles and veg all in one.

# Satay noodles with crunchy veg

3 tbsp crunchy peanut butter
3 tbsp sweet chilli sauce
2 tbsp soy sauce
300g pack straight-to-wok noodles
1 tbsp oil
a thumb-sized knob of ginger, grated
300g pack stir-fry vegetables
a handful of fresh basil leaves
25g/1oz roasted peanuts,
roughly chopped

Takes 15 minutes • Serves 4

1  Mix the peanut butter, chilli and soy sauces with 100ml/3½fl oz hot water to make a smooth satay sauce.
2  Put the noodles in a bowl and pour boiling water over them. Stir gently to separate, then drain thoroughly.
3  Heat the oil in a wok, then stir-fry the ginger and harder pieces of veg from the stir-fry mix, such as peppers, for 2 minutes. Add the noodles and the rest of the veg, then stir-fry over a high heat for 1–2 minutes until the veg are just cooked.
4  Push the veg to one side of the pan, then pour the satay sauce into the other side, tilting the pan. Bring to the boil. Mix the sauce with the stir-fry, then sprinkle over the basil leaves and peanuts to serve.

• Per serving 286 kcalories, protein 10g, carbohydrate 34g, fat 14g, saturated fat 2g, fibre 5g, sugar 6g, salt 2.29g

The parathas can be cooked several hours ahead then reheated in the oven, wrapped in foil, at 180°C/160°C fan/gas 4 for 10 minutes.

# Coriander parathas

450g/1lb chapati flour, plus extra for rolling
1 tsp salt
6 tbsp chopped fresh coriander
300ml/½ pint warm water
oil, for brushing

Takes 30 minutes • Makes 10

1  Mix together the flour, salt and coriander. Gradually add the water, mixing to make a dough – it should be neither too sticky nor too dry or it will be difficult to roll. Cut into 10 pieces and cover loosely with a tea towel.
2  Heat a cast-iron pan or griddle until hot. Lightly roll out each ball, sprinkling with a little flour to prevent sticking, into a 20cm circle. Slap the paratha on to the dry griddle and let it cook for 45 seconds–1 minute until it starts to puff, then turn over. Brush the cooked side with oil, turn over again and cook for 20 seconds. Brush the other side with oil, turn and cook for 20 seconds.
3  Remove the paratha to a plate and cover loosely with a tea towel. Repeat with the remaining dough until you have 10 parathas.

• Per paratha 187 kcalories, protein 5g, carbohydrate 37g, fat 3g, saturated fat 0.4g, fibre 2g, sugar 1g, salt 0.52g

This pilaf can be made ahead – just cool it quickly by spreading on a baking sheet before chilling, then reheat in a microwave until piping hot.

# Turmeric pilaf with golden onions

400g/14oz basmati rice
4 tbsp olive oil
1½ tsp cumin seeds
1 tsp black mustard seeds
2 large onions, halved and sliced
just under 1 tsp ground turmeric
2 red or green chillies, seeded and thinly sliced

Takes 30 minutes • Serves 6

1 Thoroughly rinse the rice until the water looks completely clear. Drain, then tip into a large pan of salted water. Bring to the boil and cook for 6 minutes until just tender. Drain well.

2 Heat the oil in a large wok and fry the seeds until they start to pop. Add the onions and cook, stirring frequently, until they are tender and golden. Stir in the turmeric and chillies, and cook for 1–2 minutes more. Add the rice and heat through, stirring, until thoroughly hot. Serve immediately.

• Per serving 323 kcalories, protein 6g, carbohydrate 60g, fat 8g, saturated fat 1g, fibre 1g, sugar 4g, salt 0.01g

A cooling raita is the perfect match for a hot and spicy curry.

# Coriander and mango raita

1 tsp cumin seeds
500g pot natural yogurt
3 tbsp chopped fresh coriander
1 ripe mango, peeled and diced
a finger-length piece of cucumber,
seeded and chopped
1 green chilli, seeded and
finely chopped
1 tsp golden caster sugar

Takes 15 minutes • Serves 6

1 Dry-roast the cumin seeds in a pan on a low heat, moving them around. After a few minutes, they will begin to change colour to a golden brown. Remove from the heat and crush coarsely using a pestle and mortar.
2 Put all the other ingredients in a bowl and stir in the crushed seeds. Season with salt to taste.

• Per serving 83 kcalories, protein 5g, carbohydrate 14g, fat 1g, saturated fat none, fibre 1g, sugar 14g, salt 0.14g

The addition of fresh coconut makes this a typically southern Indian dish.

# Spinach with coconut

50g/2oz yellow split peas or red lentils
2 tbsp vegetable oil
1 tsp mustard seeds
5 curry leaves (optional)
2 small thin red chillies
1 small onion, chopped
250g/9oz fresh spinach, shredded
flesh of ½ fresh coconut, grated

Takes 45 minutes • Serves 6

1  In a pan of boiling water, cook the split peas for about 25 minutes until they are tender but still keep their shape. Or, if you are using lentils, cook them for 15–20 minutes.
2  Meanwhile, heat the vegetable oil in a large pan, then add the mustard seeds, curry leaves (if using), whole red chillies and chopped onion; fry for 5 minutes.
3  Wash and drain the shredded spinach. Drain the split peas or lentils, then add to the pan of spices with the grated coconut and toss over the heat for another 5 minutes. Add the spinach and when it has wilted, season and serve.

• Per serving 136 kcalories, protein 4g, carbohydrate 6g, fat 11g, saturated fat 6g, fibre 2g, sugar 2g, salt 0.16g

A pakora's characteristic crisp batter comes from the gram
or chickpea flour with which it is made. Look for gram flour
in Indian stores or health food shops.

# Prawn, mango and spring onion pakoras

140g/5oz gram flour or plain flour
2 tsp garam masala
1 tsp ground turmeric
3 green chillies, seeded and finely chopped
1 small mango, peeled and chopped
4 spring onions, finely sliced
200g/8oz raw peeled prawns, chopped
vegetable oil, for deep-frying
200ml carton coconut cream
a large knob of ginger, roughly chopped
a handful of fresh coriander leaves

Takes 40 minutes • Makes 24

1  Preheat the oven to its lowest temperature. Tip the flour into a large bowl and stir in the spices and a large pinch of salt. Make a well in the middle, then gradually whisk in 100ml/3½fl oz water until you have a smooth but thick batter. Mix in the chillies, mango, spring onions and prawns.
2  Heat 5cm oil in a deep pan, then drop in spoonfuls of the mix. Fry four at a time for 3–4 minutes, until crisp and lightly golden. Drain on kitchen paper and keep warm in a low oven until ready to serve.
3  For the dip, blend the coconut cream, ginger and coriander together in a food processor until smooth. Serve in a bowl alongside the pakoras.

• Per pakora 97 kcalories, protein 3g, carbohydrate 5g, fat 7g, saturated fat 3g, fibre 1g, sugar 2g, salt 0.05g

This zingy, superhealthy salad will liven up any table.

# Peppery fennel and carrot salad

2 large carrots, cut into thin sticks or grated
2 large fennel bulbs, quartered and thinly sliced
a handful of peanuts or cashew nuts, chopped
2 tbsp olive oil
1 tsp mustard seeds
1 tsp kalonji seeds (also known as black onion or nigella seeds)
juice of 1 lemon or lime

Takes 10 minutes • Serves 6

1  Tip the carrots and fennel into a large salad bowl.
2  Toast the nuts in a hot frying pan for 3–5 minutes until golden, then tip out on to a plate and set aside. In the same pan, heat the oil and fry the mustard and kalonji seeds until they begin to pop – about 30 seconds. Pour in the lemon or lime juice and mix together to make a dressing.
3  Toss the dressing with the vegetables in the bowl, then sprinkle with the nuts to serve.

• Per serving 87 kcalories, protein 2g, carbohydrate 6g, fat 6g, saturated fat 1g, fibre 3g, sugar 5g, salt 0.05g

In Thailand green mango salad is a popular dish, but green mangoes can be hard to find – here we've swapped them for crisp green apples instead.

# Green apple salad

2 shallots, finely sliced
1 tbsp vegetable oil
5 sharp green apples, such as Granny Smith, cored and thinly sliced
6 cherry tomatoes, quartered
2 tbsp dry-roasted peanuts, crushed
a handful of fresh coriander leaves, chopped

FOR THE DRESSING
1 garlic clove, finely chopped
1 red chilli, seeded and finely chopped
1 tsp sugar
1 tbsp Thai fish sauce
juice of 2 limes

Takes 15 minutes • Serves 4

1 To make the dressing, whiz together the garlic, chilli, sugar, fish sauce and lime juice in a food processor.
2 Fry the shallots in the oil for 5 minutes or until crisp and golden brown. Remove with a slotted spoon and drain on kitchen paper.
3 Toss the apples with the tomatoes and dressing. Spoon on to plates and top with the peanuts, crisp shallots and coriander.

• Per serving 152 kcalories, protein 3g, carbohydrate 21g, fat 7g, saturated fat 1g, fibre 3g, added sugar 1.4g, salt 0.9g

Serve these simple stir-fried vegetables with some jasmine rice and a spicy Thai curry.

# Stir-fried pak choi and water chestnuts

700g/1lb 9oz mixture of pak choi and carrots
3 tbsp vegetable oil
3 garlic cloves, finely chopped
220g can water chestnuts, drained, rinsed and sliced
1 tbsp Thai fish sauce (nam pla)
2 tbsp oyster sauce
a pinch of sugar
a good pinch of white pepper

Takes 15 minutes • Serves 6

1 Roughly chop the pak choi (keep small leaves whole). Peel and slice the carrots, then halve each slice.

2 Heat the oil in a wok or large frying pan over a high heat. Stir-fry the garlic for a few seconds, then add the carrots. Stir-fry quickly for about 1 minute, then stir in the pak choi and cook for another minute. Add the water chestnuts, 3 tablespoons of water, the fish and oyster sauces, sugar and pepper. Stir quickly and cook for a further 1–2 minutes until the vegetables are lightly cooked, but still crisp. Serve immediately.

• Per serving 95 kcalories, protein 2g, carbohydrate 9g, fat 6g, saturated fat 0.7g, fibre 2g, sugar 7g, salt 1.17g

This bread is called thepla in India; serve with small bowls of natural yogurt and mango chutney.

# Indian bread with courgettes and coriander

½ tsp cumin seeds
450g/1lb courgettes, coarsely grated
175g/6oz plain flour, plus extra for rolling out
175g/6oz plain wholemeal flour
2 tsp grated ginger
a good pinch of ground turmeric
a small handful of fresh coriander, chopped
3–4 tbsp sunflower oil

Takes 1 hour • Makes 12

1  Dry-fry the cumin seeds for 1 minute in a non-stick pan until toasted.
2  Mix with the grated courgettes, flours, ginger, turmeric and coriander in a large bowl with 1 teaspoon salt. Rub in 1½ tablespoons of the oil, then slowly mix in 4–5 tablespoons cold water until a soft dough forms. Tear into 12 pieces and shape into balls.
3  Using a little extra flour, roll each piece into a thin 14cm round. Heat a griddle or heavy-based frying pan until very hot. Add one or two breads and cook for 2 minutes, patting with a clean cloth – this helps the bread cook fast. Turn the breads over and cook for around 2 minutes more.
4  Drizzle a little oil over, turn the breads again for 30–60 seconds more, then drizzle a few drops of oil on this side. Remove and repeat with the rest. Serve hot or cold.

• Per thepla 257 kcalories, protein 8g, carbohydrate 43g, fat 7g, saturated fat 1g, fibre 4g, added sugar none, salt 0.01g

An Indian-style coleslaw that's delicious served with tomato-based curries or spicy grilled meats.

# Indian summer salad

3 carrots
1 bunch of radishes
2 courgettes
½ small red onion
a small handful of fresh mint leaves

FOR THE DRESSING
1 tbsp white wine vinegar
1 tsp Dijon mustard
1 tbsp mayonnaise
2 tbsp olive oil

Takes 20 minutes • Serves 6

1 Grate the carrots into a large bowl. Thinly slice the radishes and courgettes, and finely chop the onion. Mix all the vegetables together in the bowl with the mint leaves.
2 Whisk together the vinegar, mustard and mayonnaise for the dressing until smooth, then gradually whisk in the oil. Add salt and freshly ground black pepper to taste, then drizzle over the salad and mix well.

• Per serving 79 kcalories, protein 1g, carbohydrate 5g, fat 6g, saturated fat 1g, fibre 2g, sugar 6g, salt 0.35g

Kulfi, or Indian ice cream, is popular in northern India, but ice cream like this one here is popular throughout the southern regions.

# Mango and cardamom ice cream

1.4 litres/2½ pints full-fat milk
200g/8oz golden caster sugar
1 tsp ground cardamom, or crushed seeds from about 30 pods
2 tbsp slivered pistachio nuts
1 tbsp desiccated coconut
1 medium mango, peeled and diced
crushed cardamom seeds, mango slices and fresh lime juice, to serve

Takes 1¼ hours, plus chilling and freezing • Serves 6

1  Put the milk and sugar in a pan and bring to the boil for 15 minutes, stirring constantly to prevent it bubbling over. Lower the heat and simmer, uncovered, for 35–45 minutes, stirring occasionally, until reduced by half. Stir in the ground cardamom.

2  Pour into a bowl and leave to cool to room temperature. Then churn, stirring in the nuts, coconut and mango before transferring to six cups or moulds and freezing overnight. If you don't have an ice-cream maker, freeze the cooled milk for an hour until small crystals form, then stir in the bits and transfer to the individual cups for freezing.

3  Remove the moulds from the freezer 5 minutes before serving, then turn out on to serving plates. Scatter over a little crushed cardamom, mango slices and lime juice.

• Per serving 362 kcalories, protein 9g, carbohydrate 57g, fat 12g, saturated fat 7g, fibre 2g, sugar 57g, salt 0.26g

A lassi is a refreshing, non-alcoholic Indian drink.

# Spiced and sweet lassis

2 tbsp cumin seeds
2 tbsp rosewater
85g/3oz caster sugar
500g tub low-fat natural yogurt
a few fresh coriander leaves,

Takes 15 minutes, plus cooling
Serves 6

1 Toast the cumin seeds in a non-stick frying pan for 1 minute, then set aside to cool.
2 In a small pan, mix the rosewater and sugar with 50ml/2fl oz water. Heat gently until the sugar has melted, then bubble for a minute until syrupy. Cool.
3 To serve, put the rosewater syrup, toasted cumin seeds and coriander leaves into three separate small serving bowls. Using a balloon whisk, whisk the yogurt with 450ml/16fl oz cold water until frothy. Divide among six tumblers and let everyone help themselves to either a sprinkling of cumin seeds and coriander (for a spiced lassi) or a drizzle of rosewater syrup (for a sweet lassi).

• Per serving (Spiced lassi) 115 kcalories, protein 5g, carbohydrate 22g, fat 2g, saturated fat 1g, fibre none, sugar 20g, salt 0.18g • (Sweet lassi) 99 kcalories, protein 4g, carbohydrate 20g, fat 1g, saturated fat 1g, fibre none, sugar 20g, salt 0.16g

Curries can be filling, so if you don't fancy finishing with a proper dessert just serve a few squares of this sweet treat.

# Coconut ice squares

50g/2oz sweetened condensed milk
250g/9oz icing sugar, sifted, plus extra for dusting
200g/8oz dessicated coconut
pink edible food colouring

Takes 15 minutes, plus 3 hours or overnight to set • Makes 32 squares

1 Using a wooden spoon, mix together the condensed milk and icing sugar in a large bowl. It will get very stiff. Work the coconut into the mix until it's well combined – use your hands, if you like.
2 Split the mix into two and knead a very small amount of the food colouring into one half. Dust a board with extra icing sugar, then shape each half into a smooth rectangle and place one on top of the other. Roll with a rolling pin, re-shaping with your hands every couple of rolls, until you have a rectangle of two-tone coconut ice about 3cm thick.
3 Transfer to a plate or board and leave, uncovered, for at least 3 hours (or ideally overnight) to set. Cut into 32 squares with a sharp knife and keep for up to a month in an airtight container.

• Per square 76kcalories, protein 1g, carbohydrate 10g, fat 4 g, saturated fat 3g, fibre 1g, sugar 10g, salt 0.01g

This recipe uses canned pineapple, but you could use fresh fruit, if you prefer – just slice into rings, remove the core and replace the syrup from the can with double the amount of sugar and water used here.

# Pineapple with chilli and vanilla syrup

432g can pineapple rings in syrup
50g/2oz caster sugar
1 vanilla pod, split and seeds scraped out
½ red chilli, seeded and thinly sliced
25g/1oz unsalted butter
Greek yogurt or coconut ice cream, to serve

Takes 10 minutes • Serves 4

1  Drain the pineapple, reserving the syrup. Put the syrup, 3 tablespoons of water, the sugar, vanilla pod and chilli in a small pan, and bring to the boil. Once the syrup has come to the boil, take off the heat and leave to infuse and cool.

2  Melt the butter in a non-stick pan. When the butter stops foaming and is about to turn brown, add the pineapple and brown on both sides.

3  Add the chilli syrup and bring to the boil. The butter will slightly thicken the syrup. Serve warm with Greek yogurt or ice cream.

• Per serving 166 kcalories, protein 1g, carbohydrate 31g, fat 5g, saturated fat 3g, fibre 1g, sugar 31g, salt 0.01g

These little pots are just the right size for serving after an Indian spread.

# Fruity coconut creams

50g sachet creamed coconut
500g tub 0% Greek yogurt
85g/3oz icing sugar, sifted
a few drops of vanilla extract
2 kiwi fruits
400g can pineapple chunks in juice

Takes 10 minutes, plus chilling
Serves 4

1 Dissolve the sachet of creamed coconut in 50ml/2fl oz boiling water, then leave to cool. Spoon the yogurt into a mixing bowl, then stir in the icing sugar and vanilla. Combine with the coconut mix, then spoon into individual glasses. Chill until ready to serve.
2 Peel and chop the kiwi fruit into small pieces. Drain the pineapple, then chop the chunks into small pieces. Mix the fruit together, then spoon over the top of the coconut creams to serve.

• Per serving 266 kcalories, protein 19g, carbohydrate 40g, fat 5g, saturated fat 4g, fibre 1g, sugar 39g, salt 0.16g

Desserts are rarely served in India, but this special pud often makes an appearance at Diwali celebrations.

# Poached aromatic fruits

2 oranges, peeled and segmented
2 pears, peeled, quartered lengthways and cored
100g/4oz dried figs
100g/4oz prunes
85g/3oz dried cranberries
140g/5oz caster sugar
4 cloves
3 cardamom pods
1 cinnamon stick
a few fresh mint leaves and crème fraîche, to serve

Takes 35 minutes • Serves 6

1 Put the fresh and dried fruits in a pan with just enough water to cover. Add the sugar, cloves, cardamom pods and cinnamon stick. Bring to the boil, then reduce the heat and allow the fruits to cook gently for 10–15 minutes or until they are soft. Discard the whole spice, if you like.
2 Strain off the fruit, reserving the liquid in the pan, and set aside. Place the cooking liquid back on a high heat and boil until thick and syrupy. Cool for use later or keep warm until just before serving.
3 Divide the fruit among six bowls and pour over some of the aromatic syrup. Top with mint leaves and serve with crème fraîche.

• Per serving 313 kcalories, protein 3g, carbohydrate 65g, fat 7g, saturated fat 4g, fibre 5g, sugar 65g, salt 0.06g

This luscious dessert is low in fat, but you'd never know it.

# Vanilla yogurt ice with honeyed pink grapefruit

200g/8oz golden caster sugar
1 vanilla pod, seeds scraped out
2 × 500g tubs natural yogurt

### FOR THE HONEYED PINK GRAPEFRUIT
3 pink grapefruit
4 tbsp clear honey
fresh mint leaves, to serve

Takes 30 minutes, plus 4 hours or overnight freezing • Serves 6

1 Place the sugar in a bowl, then rub in the vanilla seeds. Stir in the yogurt until the sugar dissolves. Churn the mixture in an ice-cream machine according to the manufacturer's instructions. Meanwhile, line a 1kg loaf tin with cling film. Once churned, spoon the frozen yogurt into the tin, cover and freeze for at least 4 hours or overnight. If you don't have an ice-cream machine, freeze the yogurt mixture for 4–6 hours, stirring every hour.
2 Segment the grapefruit, catching the juice in a bowl – you should get about 200ml/7fl oz. Put the juice in a pan with the honey, simmer for 10–15 minutes until thickened, gently stir in the segments, then cool.
3 Take the yogurt ice from the freezer about 10 minutes before you want to serve it. Cut into slices and serve topped with the grapefruit, honeyed sauce and mint leaves.

• Per serving 301 kcalories, protein 8g, carbohydrate 60g, fat 5g, saturated fat 3g, fibre 1g, sugar 60g, salt 0.29g

Making your own sorbet is easier than you think, and the sharpness of these currants is fantastically refreshing after a rich curry.

# Blackcurrant and mint sorbet

200g/8oz golden caster sugar
20g pack fresh mint, plus some small sprigs to decorate
750g/1lb 10oz blackcurrants
4 tbsp liquid glucose
juice of 2 lemons

Takes 35 minutes, plus 6 hours or overnight freezing • Serves 4–6

1  Make a syrup by stirring the sugar with 700ml/1¼ pints boiling water until dissolved, then steep the mint sprigs in it until cool, about 15 minutes. Discard the mint.
2  Cook the blackcurrants in the syrup with the glucose for about 5 minutes until the fruit is soft. Whiz in a food processor, then strain into a bowl through a metal sieve, pressing it through with the back of a spoon to remove the pips. Stir in the lemon juice and cool.
3  Churn in an ice-cream machine according to the manufacturer's instructions until it becomes a thick slush, then freeze for 6 hours or overnight. Or pour into a shallow freezer container and remove 3–4 times to stir it as it freezes. Remove from the freezer about 10 minutes before serving, and decorate with sprigs of fresh mint.

• Per serving (4) 301kcalories, protein 2g, carbohydrate 78g, fat none, saturated fat none, fibre 7g, added sugar 56g, salt 0.08g

An Asian twist on a classic Italian dessert – this is a stunning pudding for a special meal.

# Coconut panna cotta with pineapple salsa

2 × 400ml cans coconut milk
400ml/14fl oz full-fat milk
100g/4oz caster sugar
1 vanilla pod, split and seeds scraped out
2 × 12g sachets powdered gelatine
a handful of coconut chips, toasted

FOR THE PINEAPPLE SALSA
85g/3oz caster sugar
25g/1oz knob of ginger, thinly sliced
250g pack fresh pineapple, cut into small pieces
1 red chilli, seeded and finely chopped

Takes 25 minutes, plus 2–48 hours chilling • Serves 6

1  Put both milks, sugar, vanilla pod and seeds into a pan. Bring to the boil, then remove from the heat and infuse for 5 minutes before discarding the pod.
2  Whisk the gelatine with 200ml/7fl oz of the hot milk mixture until dissolved (return to a gentle heat if necessary). Stir into the rest of the hot milk and pour into six 200ml metal dariole moulds. Chill for at least 2 hours or up to 2 days, until firm with a slight wobble.
3  For the salsa, tip the sugar, ginger and 100ml/3½fl oz water into a small pan. Bring to the boil, simmer for 5–10 minutes until slightly syrupy. Cool, then discard the ginger.
4  To serve, dip each mould into hot water, then turn out on to a plate. Top with toasted coconut, some pineapple and chopped chilli, and drizzle with the ginger syrup.

• Per serving 418 kcalories, protein 8g, carbohydrate 44g, fat 25g, saturated fat 21g, fibre 1g, sugar 44g, salt 0.49g

This lassi is equally good served before, during or after a meal
– and can be easily doubled to serve more.

# Bonny lassis

1 mango
2 scoops mango sorbet
150ml pot natural yogurt
a splash of milk
2 tsp pistachio nuts, chopped
a few fresh mint sprigs, to serve

Takes 10 minutes • Serves 2

1  Peel and stone the mango then roughly chop the flesh. Whiz in a blender with the mango sorbet and yogurt.

2  Thin with milk until you have a drinkable consistency, then pour into two glasses and top with chopped pistachios and mint sprigs.

• Per serving 227 kcalories, protein 6g, carbohydrate 43g, fat 5g, saturated fat 2g, fibre 4g, sugar 41g, salt 0.18g

These little tropical pancakes will disappear quickly – pile on a platter with small bowls of honey and yogurt and let everyone help themselves.

# Pineapple and banana pancakes

100g/4oz fresh or drained canned pineapple
1 banana
100g/4oz self-raising flour
1 tsp baking powder
1 tsp ground cinnamon
3 tbsp light muscovado sugar
1 egg
100ml/3½fl oz milk
sunflower oil, for frying
Greek yogurt and clear honey, to serve

Takes 20 minutes • Serves 4

1  Roughly chop the pineapple and slice the banana, and set aside.

2  Tip the flour, baking powder, cinnamon and sugar into a bowl and mix well. Make a well in the centre, crack in the egg, then stir in the flour mix, adding the milk gradually to make a soft batter.

3  Stir in the pineapple and banana. Heat a little oil in a non-stick frying pan then add the batter in heaped spoonfuls, spaced well apart to allow them to spread. When bubbles appear on the surface, flip the pancakes over and cook until light golden.

4  Cook all the pancakes and keep them warm. Serve 2–3 pancakes per person with a spoonful of yogurt and a little honey drizzled over the top.

• Per serving 230 kcalories, protein 6g, carbohydrate 42g, fat 6g, saturated fat 1g, fibre 1g, added sugar 11g, salt 0.7g

If you don't have a microwave, put the rice in a pan with the coconut, sugar and 200ml/7fl oz water. Simmer gently for 30 minutes, stirring until all the liquid has been absorbed.

# Mango with sticky rice

175g/6oz Thai fragrant rice
250ml carton coconut cream
85g/3oz caster sugar
1 ripe mango, sliced, to serve

FOR THE MANGO SAUCE
1 large ripe mango, peeled and flesh cut into chunks
1 tsp fresh lime juice
2 tbsp caster sugar, or to taste

Takes 45 minutes, plus 2 hours chilling
Serves 4

1 Put the rice in a microwave-proof dish and stir in the coconut cream, caster sugar and 200ml/7fl oz water. Cover with cling film, pierce and microwave on Medium for 5 minutes.
2 Stir the rice then microwave on Defrost for a further 20–25 minutes until the liquid has been absorbed and the rice is tender and sticky.
3 Spoon the rice into an 18cm-square tin and spread out evenly in a layer. Cover and chill for about 2 hours.
4 Make the sauce by whizzing the mango chunks with the lime juice and as much sugar as you wish in a food processor until smooth.
5 Once the rice is firm, cut into 12–16 pieces. Serve with the sauce and a couple of mango slices.

• Per serving 527 kcalories, protein 7g, carbohydrate 80g, fat 22g, saturated fat 19g, fibre 3g, sugar 46g, salt 0.02g

The perfect prepare-ahead pud – leaving these to chill for a while before eating allows the flavours to merge.

# Coconut and chocolate bananas

4 bananas
50g/2oz milk chocolate
50g/2oz caster sugar
½ × 400ml can coconut milk
200ml tub crème fraîche

Takes 20 minutes, plus 1 hour
chilling • Serves 4

1 Peel the bananas and thickly slice. Roughly chop the chocolate and set aside.
2 In a frying pan, toss the bananas with half the sugar, then fry for a few minutes until the bananas are slightly caramelized and the sugar has melted. Divide the bananas among four large ramekin dishes or glasses.
3 Whisk the remaining sugar with the coconut milk and crème fraîche, then divide among the four dishes. Sprinkle over the chocolate and chill for an hour before serving.

• Per serving 478 kcalories, protein 4g, carbohydrate 46g, fat 32g, saturated fat 22g, fibre 1g, sugar 44g, salt 0.2g

This creamy dessert is called shrikhand and is very popular along the west coast of India.

# Creamy saffron yogurt

700g/1lb 9oz Greek yogurt
2 tsp green cardamom pods
100g/4oz golden caster sugar
8–10 saffron strands
1 tsp milk
1 tbsp shelled pistachio nuts, slivered, to decorate
1 large ripe mango, sliced, to serve

Takes 40 minutes • Serves 6

1  Place a piece of muslin or thick kitchen paper in a large sieve set over a large bowl. Spoon the yogurt into the sieve, cover with another piece of muslin or 2 sheets of kitchen paper and set aside at room temperature for 25–30 minutes (this is done to remove excess moisture).

2  Remove the seeds from the cardamom pods and crush them using a pestle and mortar – you will need 1 teaspoon of ground cardamom. Set aside.

3  Discard the kitchen paper or muslin, scrape the yogurt into a bowl and stir in the sugar. Mix the saffron strands with the milk, then add both to the yogurt with the ground cardamom and mix well. Divide among six small glasses, scatter with pistachio slivers and serve with fresh mango slices.

• Per serving (including serving suggestions)
204 kcalories, protein 8g, carbohydrate 21g, fat 11g, saturated fat 7g, fibre none, added sugar 18g, salt 0.22g

A deliciously sweet, gently spiced tea that is excellent at the end of a meal to aid digestion. Use a strong, full-bodied blend of tea such as Assam.

# Spiced Indian tea

400ml/14fl oz full-fat milk
½ × finger-length knob of ginger, bruised
5 cardamom pods, lightly crushed
5 rounded tsp loose Indian tea
3 tbsp caster sugar

Takes 4 minutes • Serves 6

1  Tip the full-fat milk into a large pan with 700ml/1¼ pints water. Add the ginger and cardamom pods, and bring to the boil. Stir in the tea, then simmer for 2–3 minutes only.
2  Strain, then stir in the sugar before serving in small cups.

• Per serving 77 kcalories, protein 2g, carbohydrate 11g, fat 3g, saturated fat 2g, fibre none, sugar 11g, salt 0.07g

# Index

# Picture and recipe credits

BBC *Good Food* magazine would like to thank the following people for providing photos. While every effort has been made to trace and acknowledge all photographers, we should like to apologize should there be any errors or omissions.

Marie-Louise Avery p27, p189; Iain Bagwell p41, p59; Steve Baxter p99, p175; Peter Cassidy p25, p39, p73, p143, p201; Jean Cazals p111, p117, p135, p177, p205; Ken Field p33; Dean Grannan p103; Will Heap p17, p129; Gareth Morgans p11, p13, p55, p57, p63, p65, p161, p191; David Munns p47, p67, p91, p105, p115, p121, p125, p141, p147, p153, p163, p167, p169, p181, p182, p193, p203, p211; Myles New p19, p37, p61, p71, p85, p101, p149, p151, p173; Lis Parsons p123, p127, p137, p159, p164, p171, p195, p199; William Reavell p155; Craig Robertson p207; Simon Smith p43, p95; Roger Stowell p15, p21, p23, p35, p45, p49, p51, p69, p77, p79, p89, p93, p107, p113, p119, p131; Yuki Sugiura p145; Martin Thompson p109, p179, p185, p209; Dawie Verwey p75; Simon Walton p87; Philip Webb p31, p81, p133, p139, p157, p197; Simon Wheeler p53, p83; Kate Whitaker p97; Elizabeth Zeschin p29, p187

All the recipes in this book were created by the editorial team at *Good Food* and by regular contributors to the magazine.